Lonsdale SCIENCE REVISION GUIDES

INTRODUCTION ...

This revision guide is matched perfectly to AQA Single Award Science for both SPECIFICATION A (MODULAR) and SPECIFICATION B (COORDINATED). It contains everything the pupils need, ... and nothing more, as one would expect from a highly refined revision text.

For Pupils Following The Modular Specification

- Material in the first three modules which may be tested again in the terminal examination is outlined by red boxes. Similarly, throughout this volume, material which is HIGHER TIER only is indicated by the presence of a pale blue background.

- Page 76 of this guide applies ONLY to the Coordinated Specification and as such does not need to be revised by pupils studying the Modular course.

For Pupils Following The Coordinated Specification

- Although the guide is divided into six modules they cover the entire content required by the Coordinated Specification in respect of Life Processes and Living Things (Biology), Materials and their Properties (Chemistry) and Physical Processes (Physics). However page 35 of the guide applies ONLY to the Modular Specification and as such does not need to be revised by pupils following the Coordinated course.

- As in the Modular specification, material which is HIGHER TIER only is indicated by the presence of a pale blue background. **Pupils following the Coordinated course should ignore <u>all</u> the red boxes in this guide.**

And Finally ...

This guide is intended as a source of first rate revision material for GSCE students but it is also our hope that it eases the burden of overworked Science Departments.

Mary James

Mary James – **Editor**

The Tested Modules

Covered In Class   Revised   Revised   Page No.

Life And Living Processes

Materials And Reactions

Energy And Electricity

The Terminal Modules

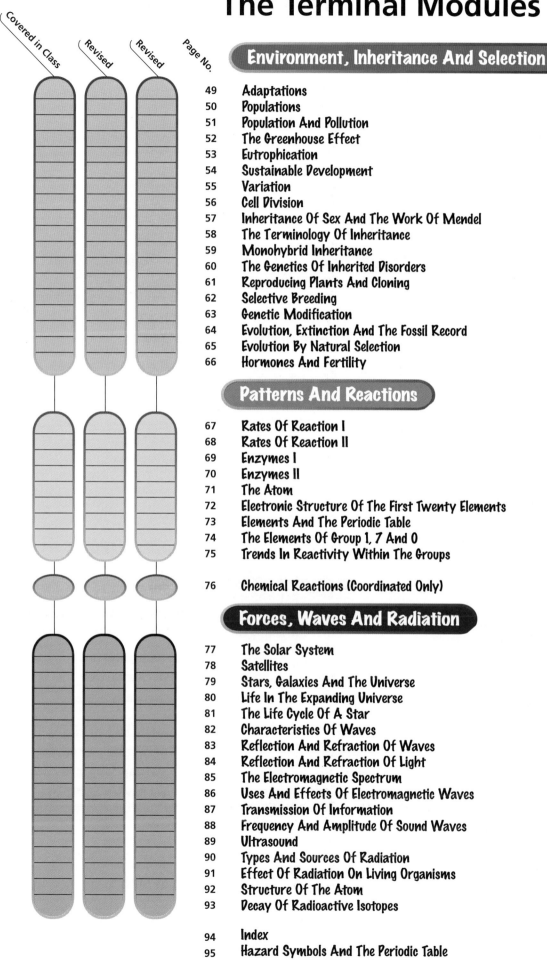

An Example Of A Human Cell

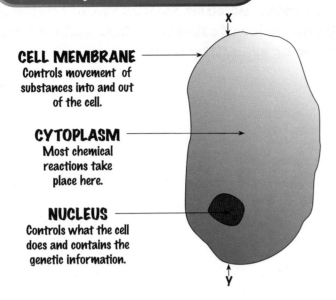

CELL MEMBRANE
Controls movement of substances into and out of the cell.

CYTOPLASM
Most chemical reactions take place here.

NUCLEUS
Controls what the cell does and contains the genetic information.

X

Y

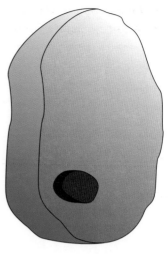

This shows the cell as it would look if it had been cut along the line XY.

Most cells are made up of water containing dissolved substances. These substances are usually in the process of being made into something which the cell needs. This involves chemical reactions controlled by ENZYMES. These often occur in structures called MITOCHONDRIA in the cytoplasm where most of the energy is released via the chemical reactions which occur in RESPIRATION.

Types Of Human Cell

Some cells are highly SPECIALISED to do a particular job ...

MASSIVE FOOD RESERVES FOR THE DEVELOPING EMBRYO.

The OVUM or egg cell is much larger than other cells so that it can carry massive food reserves for the developing embryo.

The SPERM CELL is the most mobile cell because of its tail. It has to travel from the vagina to the ovum.

RED BLOOD CELLS lose their nucleus so that they can be packed full of haemoglobin in order to carry lots of oxygen.

WHITE BLOOD CELLS can change their shape in order to engulf and destroy microbes which have invaded the body.

EPITHELIAL CELLS are flattened in shape and joined together at the edges, so that they can form covering layers eg. skin.

GLANDULAR CELLS have a large cavity into which substances are emptied before being released. They are found in the digestive system.

CILIATED EPITHELIAL CELLS move mucus along our windpipe, trapping and carrying away debris which we have breathed in.

NERVE CELLS (Neurones) have long slender processes which can carry nerve impulses over distances as long as 1 metre.

CELLS TISSUES ORGANS ORGAN SYSTEMS ORGANISM

The DIGESTIVE SYSTEM is really made up of a long MUSCULAR TUBE in which ENZYMES speed up (catalyse) the breakdown of LARGE INSOLUBLE MOLECULES eg. starch, proteins and fats into SMALLER SOLUBLE MOLECULES so that they can pass through the walls of the small intestine and into the bloodstream. Reabsorption of water takes place in the large intestine leaving indigestible food which leaves the body as faeces via the anus.

The Human Digestive System

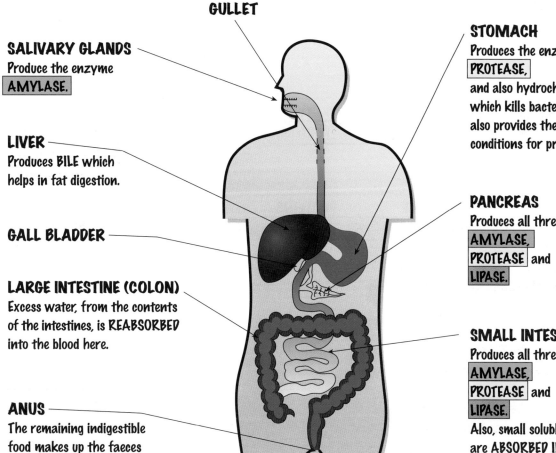

GULLET

SALIVARY GLANDS
Produce the enzyme
AMYLASE.

LIVER
Produces BILE which
helps in fat digestion.

GALL BLADDER

LARGE INTESTINE (COLON)
Excess water, from the contents
of the intestines, is REABSORBED
into the blood here.

ANUS
The remaining indigestible
food makes up the faeces
which leave the body here.

STOMACH
Produces the enzyme
PROTEASE,
and also hydrochloric acid
which kills bacteria, and
also provides the ideal
conditions for protease.

PANCREAS
Produces all three enzymes ...
AMYLASE,
PROTEASE and
LIPASE.

SMALL INTESTINE (ILEUM)
Produces all three enzymes
AMYLASE,
PROTEASE and
LIPASE.
Also, small soluble molecules
are ABSORBED INTO THE
BLOODSTREAM.

The Function Of Bile

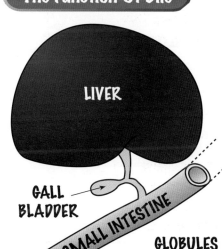

LIVER

GALL
BLADDER

SMALL INTESTINE

Bile is produced in the LIVER and then stored in the GALL BLADDER ...
... before being released into the SMALL INTESTINE.
Bile has 2 functions ...

(1) ... it neutralises the acid, which was added to food in the stomach, to produce ALKALINE conditions in which the enzymes of the small intestine work best.

(2) ... it EMULSIFIES fats ie. it breaks large drops of fat into small droplets to increase their surface area. This enables the lipase enzymes to work much faster.

GLOBULES
OF FAT   BILE   DROPLETS OF FAT

Enzyme Summary

Three enzymes PROTEASE, LIPASE and AMYLASE are produced in four separate regions of the digestive system. They digest Proteins, Fats and Carbohydrates to produce molecules which can be absorbed.

SALIVARY GLANDS

| AMYLASE | CARBOHYDRATES → | SUGARS |

STOMACH

| PROTEASE | PROTEINS → | AMINO ACIDS |

PANCREAS
(These enzymes are released into the small intestine).

AMYLASE	CARBOHYDRATES →	SUGARS
PROTEASE	PROTEINS →	AMINO ACIDS
LIPASE	LIPIDS (fats & oils) →	FATTY ACIDS + GLYCEROL

SMALL INTESTINE

AMYLASE	CARBOHYDRATES →	SUGARS
PROTEASE	PROTEINS →	AMINO ACIDS
LIPASE	LIPIDS (fats & oils) →	FATTY ACIDS + GLYCEROL

Absorption In The Small Intestine

The three enzymes catalyse the breakdown of LARGE INSOLUBLE MOLECULES into SMALL SOLUBLE MOLECULES which then diffuse through the walls of the small intestine into the bloodstream.

PROTEINS

CARBOHYDRATES (ie. starch)

LIPIDS (ie. fats and oils)

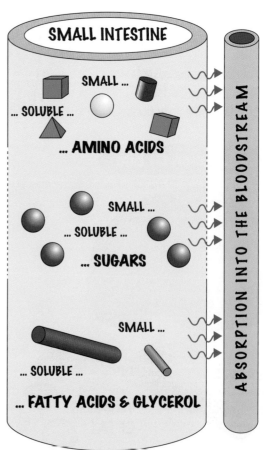

If blood is allowed to stand without clotting, it separates out into its 4 components ...

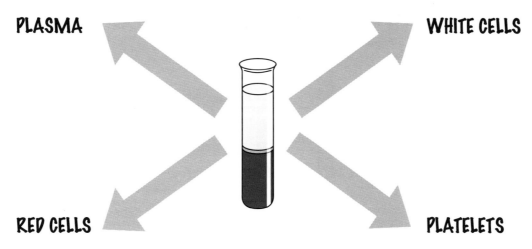

PLASMA

WHITE CELLS

RED CELLS

PLATELETS

Plasma

PLASMA is a straw-coloured liquid which transports ...
* ... carbon dioxide from the organs to the lungs ...
* ... soluble products of digestion from the small intestine to the organs ...
* ... other wastes (eg. urea) from the liver to the kidneys.

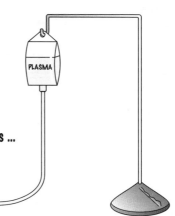

PLASMA

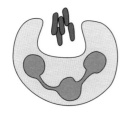 

White Cells

WHITE CELLS have a nucleus which is variable in shape.
* Some engulf invading microbes to defend the body ...
  ... while others produce ANTIBODIES to attack them.
* There's 1 white cell for every 600 red cells!!

Platelets

PLATELETS are tiny pieces of cell which have no nucleus.
* They clump together when a blood vessel is damaged ...
  ... and form a meshwork of fibres ...
  ... to produce a CLOT.

Red Cells

RED CELLS transport OXYGEN from the lungs to the organs.

* They have NO NUCLEUS so that they can contain lots of HAEMOGLOBIN, (a red pigment which can carry oxygen).
* In the lungs HAEMOGLOBIN combines with oxygen to form OXYHAEMOGLOBIN. In other organs OXYHAEMOGLOBIN splits up into HAEMOGLOBIN plus OXYGEN.

Bacteria And Viruses

These are the two main types of microorganism which may affect health.

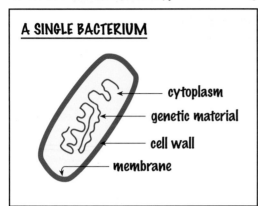

A SINGLE BACTERIUM

cytoplasm
genetic material
cell wall
membrane

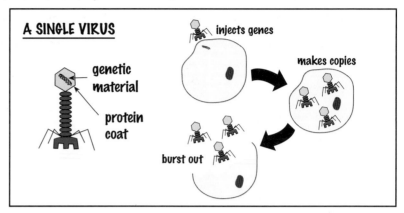

A SINGLE VIRUS

genetic material
protein coat

injects genes
makes copies
burst out

A Comparison Between Bacteria And Viruses

BACTERIA	VIRUSES
Consist of CYTOPLASM and a MEMBRANE surrounded by a CELL WALL.	Have a simple PROTEIN COAT. No membrane or cell wall.
The genetic material is NOT contained within a NUCLEUS.	The genetic material is NOT contained within a NUCLEUS.
Very small.	Even smaller.
Reproduce very quickly.	Reproduce very quickly - BUT ONLY INSIDE LIVING CELLS, WHICH ARE THEN DAMAGED. (see above)
Can produce TOXINS (poisons) which make us feel ill.	Can produce TOXINS (poisons) which make us feel ill.
Responsible for diseases such as TETANUS, CHOLERA, TUBERCULOSIS.	Responsible for diseases such as COLDS, FLU, MEASLES, POLIO.

- Microorganisms can ENTER THE BODY through NATURAL OPENINGS (eg. the nose or mouth) ...
  ... and through BREAKS IN THE SKIN (cuts, bites).
- If LARGE NUMBERS OF MICROORGANISMS enter the body due to UNHYGIENIC CONDITIONS ...
  ... or contact with INFECTED PEOPLE ...
  ... the MICROORGANISMS can REPRODUCE RAPIDLY and make the person unwell.

Our Defence Against Microorganisms

1 The blood produces CLOTS that seal cuts. ——————————→

2 The BREATHING ORGANS produce a STICKY, LIQUID MUCUS, ————
   which covers the lining of these organs and traps microorganisms.

3 The SKIN acts as a barrier to invading microorganisms. ————→

4 The white cells
   - When a microorganism invades the body and starts to multiply ...
   - ... the body's WHITE CELLS multiply in response. (see next page).

A white cell ingesting (eating) microorganisms.

The WHITE BLOOD CELLS form part of the body's IMMUNE SYSTEM.
White blood cells work by ...

1 INGESTING MICROORGANISMS.

2 PRODUCING ANTITOXINS to NEUTRALISE TOXINS produced by the microorganisms.

3 PRODUCING ANTIBODIES to DESTROY PARTICULAR MICROORGANISMS.

Ingesting Microorganisms

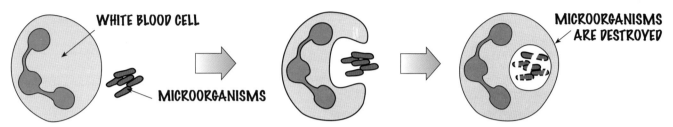

Microorganisms invade the body ...

... the white blood cell starts to surround the microorganisms.

The microorganisms are INGESTED by the white blood cell.

Producing Antitoxins

White blood cells produce ANTITOXINS which NEUTRALISE HARMFUL TOXINS (poisons) produced by microorganisms.

Producing Antibodies

• WHITE BLOOD CELLS recognise the microorganisms as ANTIGENS (foreign bodies) ...
  ... and produce ANTIBODIES to destroy the ANTIGENS. (Often by making them clump together!).

• The reason we feel ILL is because it takes TIME for the WHITE BLOOD CELLS to produce ANTIBODIES to the microorganisms.

• The PRODUCTION OF ANTIBODIES is much faster if a person has already had the infectious disease. The WHITE BLOOD CELLS seem to 'remember' the antigen and in the future can produce ANTIBODIES more rapidly providing the person with a NATURAL IMMUNITY.

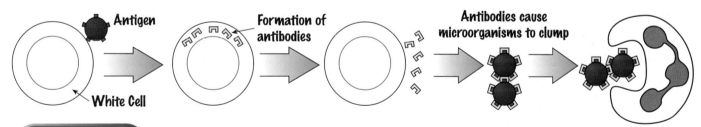

Vaccination

A person can acquire immunity to a particular disease by being vaccinated ...

STEP 1: A WEAKENED or DEAD ANTIGEN is injected into a person.

STEP 2: The body PRODUCES ANTIBODIES to fight the antigen.

STEP 3: The body now has an acquired immunity to this particular antigen since the white blood cells are now sensitised to it and will therefore respond to any future infection by producing antibodies very quickly.

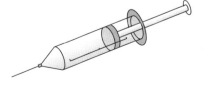

Components Of The Nervous System

- The nervous system consists of the BRAIN, the SPINAL CORD, the SPINAL NERVES and RECEPTORS.
- It allows organisms to REACT TO THEIR SURROUNDINGS and ...
  ... to COORDINATE THEIR BEHAVIOUR.
- The FIVE SENSES, namely SEEING, HEARING, TASTING, SMELLING and TOUCHING play a very important part in these processes, in which information from receptors passes along neurones to the brain which coordinates the response.

NERVOUS SYSTEM

| BRAIN | SPINAL CORD | RELAY NEURONES | SENSORY NEURONES | MOTOR NEURONES | RECEPTORS |

The Central Nervous System (C.N.S)   These make up the spinal nerves.   Respond to stimuli.

BRAIN   SPINAL CORD   SPINAL NERVES

The Three Types Of Nerve Cell (Neurone)

1 MOTOR NEURONE — DIRECTION OF IMPULSE → (away from cell body)

2 SENSORY NEURONE — DIRECTION OF IMPULSE → (towards cell body)

3 RELAY NEURONE

NEURONES are SPECIALLY ADAPTED CELLS that can carry an ELECTRICAL SIGNAL. eg. a NERVE IMPULSE.

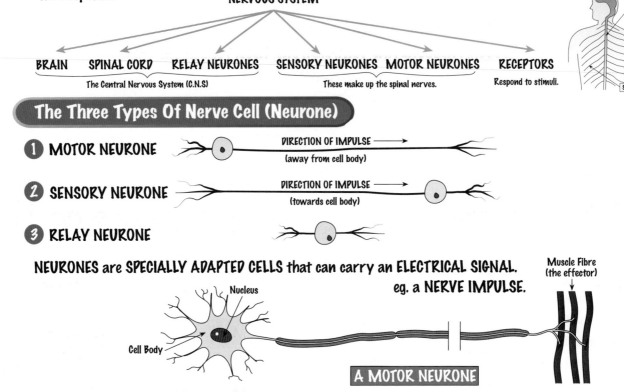

Nucleus

Cell Body

A MOTOR NEURONE

Muscle Fibre (the effector)

They are ELONGATED (long) to MAKE CONNECTIONS from one part of the body to another.
They have BRANCHED ENDINGS which allow a SINGLE NEURONE to act on MANY MUSCLE FIBRES.
The cell body has many connections to allow communication with other neurones.

Simple Reflex Action

Some responses to stimuli are designed to prevent injury to the body. When certain receptors are stimulated they cause a very fast, automatic response to the presence of danger. These are called simple reflexes and involve both sensory and motor neurones. The basic pathway for a simple reflex is shown below ...

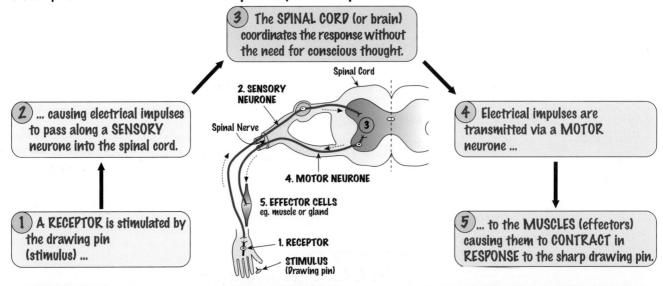

3 The SPINAL CORD (or brain) coordinates the response without the need for conscious thought.

Spinal Cord

2. SENSORY NEURONE

Spinal Nerve

2 ... causing electrical impulses to pass along a SENSORY neurone into the spinal cord.

4 Electrical impulses are transmitted via a MOTOR neurone ...

4. MOTOR NEURONE

5. EFFECTOR CELLS eg. muscle or gland

1 A RECEPTOR is stimulated by the drawing pin (stimulus) ...

1. RECEPTOR

STIMULUS (Drawing pin)

5 ... to the MUSCLES (effectors) causing them to CONTRACT in RESPONSE to the sharp drawing pin.

Types Of Receptor

- **LIGHT** RECEPTORS IN THE EYES.

- **SOUND** RECEPTORS IN THE EARS.

- **CHANGES OF POSITION** RECEPTORS IN THE EARS (for balance).

- **TASTE** RECEPTORS ON THE TONGUE.

- **SMELL** RECEPTORS IN THE NOSE.

- **TOUCH, PRESSURE AND TEMPERATURE** RECEPTORS IN THE SKIN.

The pathway for receiving information and then acting upon it is:

| STIMULUS | ⟹ | RECEPTOR | ⟹ | COORDINATOR (ANALYSER) | ⟹ | EFFECTOR | ⟹ | RESPONSE |

The coordinator is the central nervous system, to which impulses are transmitted via the spinal nerves.

Examples Of Responses To Stimuli

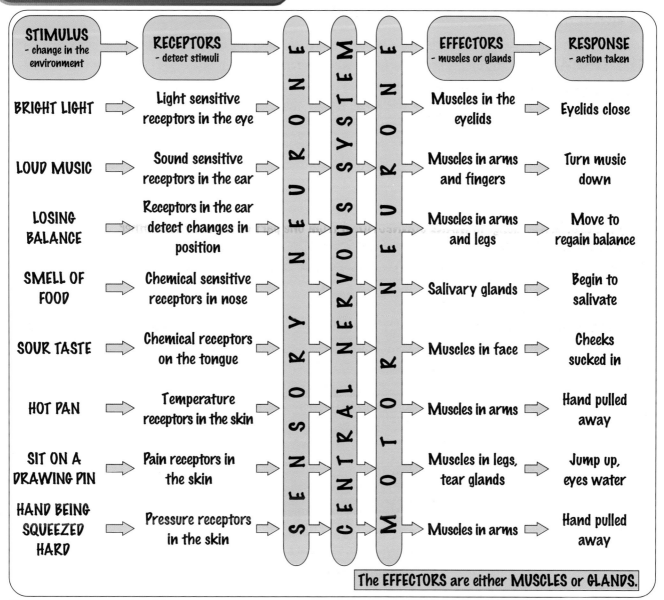

STIMULUS - change in the environment	RECEPTORS - detect stimuli	SENSORY NEURONE	CENTRAL NERVOUS SYSTEM	MOTOR NEURONE	EFFECTORS - muscles or glands	RESPONSE - action taken
BRIGHT LIGHT	Light sensitive receptors in the eye				Muscles in the eyelids	Eyelids close
LOUD MUSIC	Sound sensitive receptors in the ear				Muscles in arms and fingers	Turn music down
LOSING BALANCE	Receptors in the ear detect changes in position				Muscles in arms and legs	Move to regain balance
SMELL OF FOOD	Chemical sensitive receptors in nose				Salivary glands	Begin to salivate
SOUR TASTE	Chemical receptors on the tongue				Muscles in face	Cheeks sucked in
HOT PAN	Temperature receptors in the skin				Muscles in arms	Hand pulled away
SIT ON A DRAWING PIN	Pain receptors in the skin				Muscles in legs, tear glands	Jump up, eyes water
HAND BEING SQUEEZED HARD	Pressure receptors in the skin				Muscles in arms	Hand pulled away

The EFFECTORS are either MUSCLES or GLANDS.

These responses can be either ...

... CONSCIOUS RESPONSES, or ...

... REFLEX RESPONSES (see next page).

Conscious Action

After receiving a stimulus the body can make a considered response, ie. it acts consciously in making its response

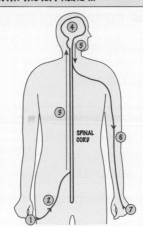

4 The brain (part of the Central Nervous System) thinks about this and decides to flick the insect away with the left hand ...

3 ... spinal cord (part of the Central Nervous System). Here, another SENSORY NEURONE carries the impulse to the brain.

2 ... these cause an impulse to travel along a SENSORY NEURONE to the ...

1 RECEPTORS in the skin of your thigh detect an insect crawling on you ...

5 An impulse is sent down a MOTOR NEURONE in the spinal cord ...

6 ... and causes an impulse to be sent out of the spinal cord via another MOTOR NEURONE ...

7 ... to a muscle (an EFFECTOR) in the hand. This causes the hand to move and flick away the insect (a RESPONSE).

SPINAL CORD

Reflex Action

Sometimes 'Conscious Action' would be too slow to prevent harm to the body eg. putting your hand on a hot plate! 'Reflex Action' speeds up the response time by missing out the brain (steps **3** ⇨ **5** in the diagram above) completely. The spinal cord acts as the coordinator and passes impulses directly from a sensory neurone to a motor neurone via a RELAY NEURONE which 'short-circuits' the brain.

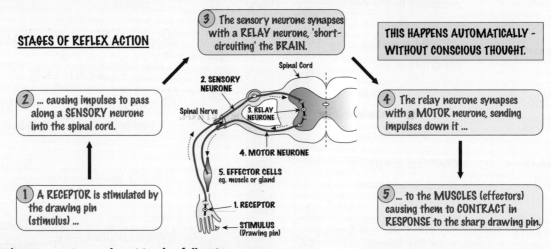

STAGES OF REFLEX ACTION

3 The sensory neurone synapses with a RELAY neurone, 'short-circuiting' the BRAIN.

THIS HAPPENS AUTOMATICALLY - WITHOUT CONSCIOUS THOUGHT.

2 ... causing impulses to pass along a SENSORY neurone into the spinal cord.

1 A RECEPTOR is stimulated by the drawing pin (stimulus) ...

4 The relay neurone synapses with a MOTOR neurone, sending impulses down it ...

5 ... to the MUSCLES (effectors) causing them to CONTRACT in RESPONSE to the sharp drawing pin.

Spinal Cord

2. SENSORY NEURONE

Spinal Nerve

3. RELAY NEURONE

4. MOTOR NEURONE

5. EFFECTOR CELLS eg. muscle or gland

1. RECEPTOR

STIMULUS (Drawing pin)

This pathway can be analysed in the following way:

STIMULUS	⇨	RECEPTOR	⇨	SENSORY NEURONE	⇨	COORDINATOR (ANALYSER)	⇨	MOTOR NEURONE	⇨	EFFECTOR	⇨	RESPONSE
Drawing pin		Pain receptor		Nerve from receptor		Relay neurone in spinal cord		Nerve to muscle		Muscle In Hand		Withdraw hand

Connections Between Neurones

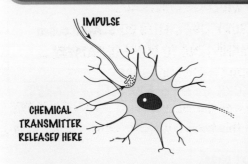

IMPULSE

CHEMICAL TRANSMITTER RELEASED HERE

- Neurones do not touch each other ...
- ... there is a very small gap between them called a SYNAPSE.
- When an electrical impulse from a neurone reaches this gap, a chemical transmitter is released which activates receptors on the neurone concerned.
- This causes an impulse to be generated in this neurone.
- The chemical transmitter is then immediately destroyed.

The Structure Of The Eye

The eye is quite a complicated sense organ which focuses light onto light-sensitive receptor cells in the retina. These are then stimulated and cause nerve impulses to pass along sensory neurones to the brain.

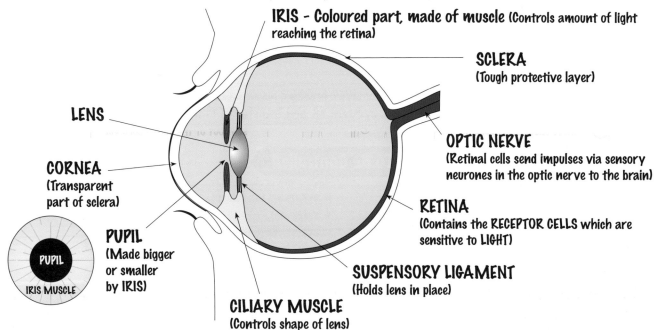

IRIS - Coloured part, made of muscle (Controls amount of light reaching the retina)

SCLERA (Tough protective layer)

LENS

OPTIC NERVE (Retinal cells send impulses via sensory neurones in the optic nerve to the brain)

CORNEA (Transparent part of sclera)

RETINA (Contains the RECEPTOR CELLS which are sensitive to LIGHT)

PUPIL (Made bigger or smaller by IRIS)

SUSPENSORY LIGAMENT (Holds lens in place)

CILIARY MUSCLE (Controls shape of lens)

PUPIL
IRIS MUSCLE

The CORNEA and the LENS focus rays of light ...
... so that an IMAGE is formed on the RETINA.

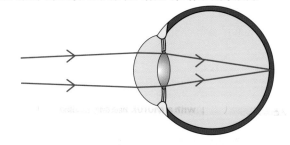

Rays of light are BENT (REFRACTED) BY THE CORNEA. The rays of light are then ...
... further BENT (REFRACTED) BY THE LENS ...
... to produce a CLEAR IMAGE ...
... on the RETINA.

Focusing On Objects At Different Distances

DISTANT OBJECT
- CILIARY MUSCLES RELAX.
- SUSPENSORY LIGAMENTS PULL TIGHT.
- LENS IS PULLED 'THINNER', and ...
- ... LIGHT ISN'T BENT AS MUCH.

NEAR OBJECT
- CILIARY MUSCLES CONTRACT.
- SUSPENSORY LIGAMENTS GO SLACK ...
- ... ALLOWING LENS TO BECOME 'FATTER', ...
- ... BENDING LIGHT MUCH MORE.

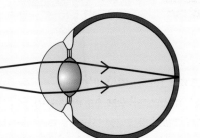

It's important to understand that the FLUID in the eye retains the shape of the eye and keeps the SUSPENSORY LIGAMENTS TIGHT. The CILIARY MUSCLES have to work to overcome this tension which is why eyes get tired after lots of focusing on near objects, eg. reading.

Humans need to remove waste products from their body to keep their INTERNAL ENVIRONMENT relatively CONSTANT. Humans need to be at just the right temperature and have just the right amount of water and sugar in the bloodstream.

Waste Products Which Have To Be Removed

CARBON DIOXIDE	• Produced by RESPIRATION. Removed via the LUNGS when we breathe out.
UREA	• Produced by LIVER breaking down excess amino acids. • Removed by KIDNEYS, and transferred to the bladder before being released.

Internal Conditions Which Have To Be Controlled

WATER CONTENT	Water lost by:-	• breathing via lungs • sweating • excess via kidneys in urine
	Water gained by:-	• drinking
ION CONTENT (Sodium, Potassium etc.)	Ions are lost by:-	• sweating • excess via kidneys in urine
	Ions are gained by:-	• eating • drinking
TEMPERATURE (Ideally at 37°C) - because this is the temperature at which ENZYMES work best!	Temperature increased by:-	• shivering • 'shutting down' skin capillaries
	Temperature decreased by:-	• sweating • 'opening up' skin capillaries

The Mechanisms And Organs Involved In These Processes

Many processes within the body (including control of some of the above internal conditions) are coordinated by HORMONES.

These are ...
- CHEMICAL SUBSTANCES, produced by GLANDS ...
- ... which are transported to their TARGET ORGANS by the BLOODSTREAM.

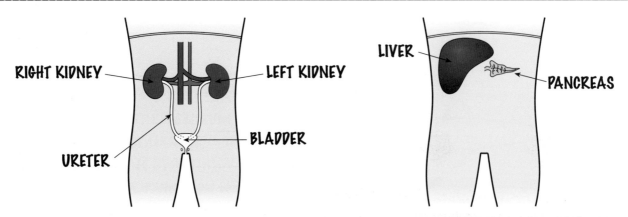

Some of the key organs involved in the control of internal conditions are the KIDNEYS, the LIVER, the PANCREAS, and the SKIN. We've shown the positions of these (except skin!) in the diagrams above and we'll look more closely at them on the next two pages.

You don't need to understand the structure of the kidney but you do need to know how it works.

- Firstly, it is made up of two important tissues, BLOOD VESSELS and TUBULES.
- BLOOD VESSELS take the blood through the kidney where unwanted substances ...
- ... end up in millions of tiny TUBULES which eventually join together to form one tube ...
- ... the URETER which leaves the kidney and ends up at the BLADDER.

THE KIDNEY REGULATES THE AMOUNT OF WATER AND IONS IN THE BLOOD AND REMOVES <u>ALL</u> UREA.

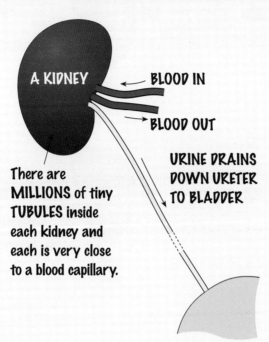

A KIDNEY

← BLOOD IN

→ BLOOD OUT

URINE DRAINS DOWN URETER TO BLADDER

There are MILLIONS of tiny TUBULES inside each kidney and each is very close to a blood capillary.

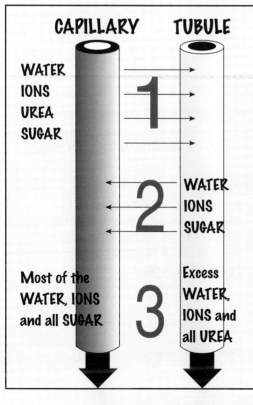

CAPILLARY   TUBULE

WATER
IONS
UREA
SUGAR

1

ULTRAFILTRATION
Lots of water plus all the small molecules are squeezed out of the blood, under pressure, into the tubules.

2

WATER
IONS
SUGAR

SELECTIVE REABSORPTION
The useful substances are reabsorbed into the blood from the tubules.

Most of the WATER, IONS and all SUGAR

3

Excess WATER, IONS and all UREA

EXCRETION OF WASTE
Excess water, ions and all the urea now pass to the bladder in the form of urine and are eventually released from the body.

So, ... in principle there are THREE STAGES to learn ...

❶ ... nearly everything is SQUEEZED OUT of the blood into the TUBULES ...

❷ ... the substances we want to keep are REABSORBED back into the blood ...

❸ ... unwanted substances are RELEASED as URINE.

Control Of Water Content – Effect Of A.D.H. On The Kidney

The amount of water reabsorbed in stage 2 on the previous page, is controlled by a hormone, A.D.H., which is produced by the PITUITARY GLAND in the brain. Everything you need to know is in this little flow diagram:-

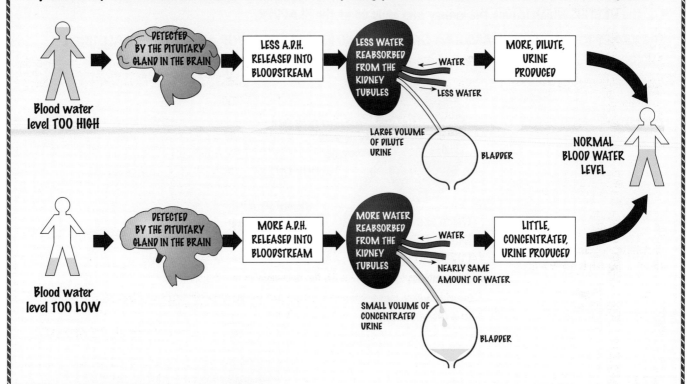

Control Of Body Temperature

This is controlled by the NERVOUS SYSTEM.

- The CORE TEMPERATURE of the body should be kept at around 37°C (best for enzymes!).
- MONITORING AND CONTROL is done by the THERMOREGULATORY CENTRE in the BRAIN ...
  ... which has receptors which are sensitive to the temperature of the blood flowing through it.
- There are also temperature receptors in the skin which provide information about skin temperature.

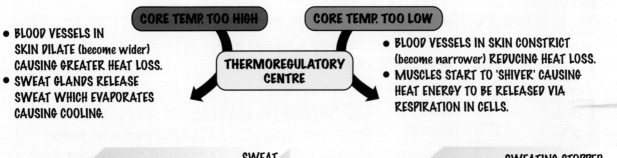

- BLOOD VESSELS IN SKIN DILATE (become wider) CAUSING GREATER HEAT LOSS.
- SWEAT GLANDS RELEASE SWEAT WHICH EVAPORATES CAUSING COOLING.

- BLOOD VESSELS IN SKIN CONSTRICT (become narrower) REDUCING HEAT LOSS.
- MUSCLES START TO 'SHIVER' CAUSING HEAT ENERGY TO BE RELEASED VIA RESPIRATION IN CELLS.

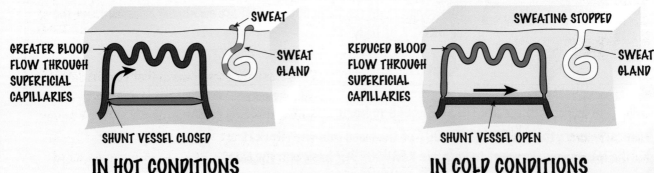

IN HOT CONDITIONS   IN COLD CONDITIONS

DRUGS are chemical substances which ALTER THE WAY THE BODY WORKS.
Some drugs can be obtained from LIVING THINGS, others are SYNTHETIC (MAN-MADE).
Some drugs are called MEDICINES and these are taken to CURE ILLNESSES or EASE THE SYMPTOMS produced during an illness. Examples include PAIN-KILLERS and ANTIBIOTICS (which destroy bacteria and some other microorganisms).

Alcohol, Tobacco And Solvents

NAME OF DRUG	FURTHER NOTES
ALCOHOL Contains the chemical ethanol.	• ALCOHOL is a DEPRESSANT and causes SLOW REACTIONS. • ALCOHOL can lead to a LACK OF SELF CONTROL. • EXCESS can lead to UNCONSCIOUSNESS and even COMA or DEATH. • The LONG TERM effects of ALCOHOL can be LIVER DAMAGE (due to the liver removing the toxic alcohol from the body) or BRAIN DAMAGE.
TOBACCO Contains the chemicals Tar Carbon Monoxide Nicotine (which is addictive)	TOBACCO is a MAJOR CAUSE of HEALTH PROBLEMS: • EMPHYSEMA - alveoli damage due to excessive coughing. • BRONCHITIS - increased infection due to INCREASED mucus production. • PROBLEMS IN PREGNANCY - Tobacco smoke contains carbon monoxide which combines irreversibly with the haemoglobin in red blood cells. This reduces the oxygen-carrying capacity of the blood. In pregnant women this can deprive a foetus of oxygen and lead to a low birth mass. • ARTERIAL and HEART DISEASE - damage to blood vessels which can lead to HEART ATTACKS, STROKES and even AMPUTATIONS.
SOLVENTS Different kinds of vapours are given off by solvents.	• SOLVENTS lead to SLOWED REACTIONS and HALLUCINATIONS. • SOLVENTS can affect a person's BEHAVIOUR and cause CHARACTER CHANGES. • SOLVENTS may cause PERMANENT DAMAGE to the LUNGS, LIVER, BRAIN or KIDNEYS.

People may become dependent or ADDICTED to certain drugs and may therefore suffer WITHDRAWAL SYMPTOMS without them. These may be psychological or physical (such as sweating, shaking, feeling sick or vomiting.)

The Link Between Lung Cancer And Smoking

The marked increase in deaths from lung cancer during the 1940's and 1950's prompted scientists to investigate the cause by monitoring a group of smokers and a group of non-smokers over a long period of time. This study showed that smokers were more likely to get lung cancer than non-smokers, and that the more a person smoked, the greater their chances of getting lung cancer.
The non-smokers in this study are called the control group and as far as possible would be in the same age range and same occupational groups as the smokers. In other words, ideally you want the control group to differ from the smoking group only because they don't smoke.

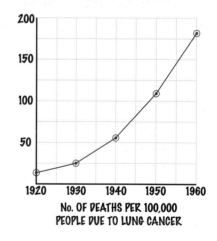

No. OF DEATHS PER 100,000 PEOPLE DUE TO LUNG CANCER

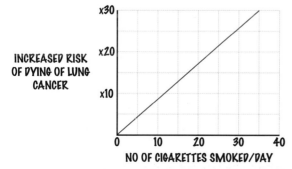

INCREASED RISK OF DYING OF LUNG CANCER

NO OF CIGARETTES SMOKED/DAY

Being a smoker doesn't mean that you will definitely get lung cancer any more than being a non-smoker means that you definitely won't get it. However, your chances are increased, and the more you smoke the greater your chances are increased.

The Periodic Table

The chemical elements can be arranged in order of their RELATIVE ATOMIC MASSES. The list can then be arranged in rows so that elements with similar properties are in the same columns, or GROUPS.
This forms the basis of the PERIODIC TABLE ...

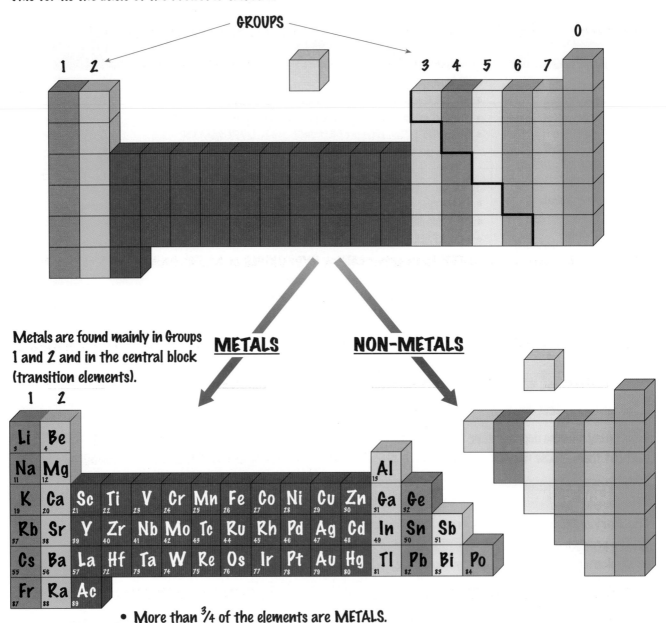

Metals are found mainly in Groups 1 and 2 and in the central block (transition elements).

METALS   **NON-METALS**

• More than ³/₄ of the elements are METALS.

In the modern Periodic Table, the elements are arranged in order of proton number since arranging them in order of relative atomic mass results in some oddities such as argon ending up in Group 1 while potassium goes to Group 0!! (instead of the other way round!).

Some Common Metals

The Periodic Table above shows the symbols for all the metallic elements.
The ones you should be familiar with are ...
LITHIUM Li, SODIUM Na, POTASSIUM K, MAGNESIUM Mg, CALCIUM Ca, IRON Fe, COPPER Cu, ZINC Zn, ALUMINIUM Al, GOLD Au, LEAD Pb.

Reaction Of Metals With Oxygen

• Metals which react with OXYGEN from the AIR form METAL OXIDES.

$$METAL + OXYGEN \longrightarrow METAL\ OXIDE$$

• Some metals react more vigorously than others. If we were to heat four different metals in air ...

| SODIUM ... | MAGNESIUM ... | COPPER ... | SILVER ... |

... BURNS VERY EASILY   ... BURNS BRIGHTLY   ... SLOW REACTION   ... NO REACTION

Reaction Of Metals With Water

• Metals which react with WATER form either METAL HYDROXIDES or METAL OXIDES and HYDROGEN.

$$METAL + WATER \longrightarrow METAL\ HYDROXIDE\ or\ METAL\ OXIDE + HYDROGEN$$

• Yet again some metals react more vigorously than others. If we were to add four different metals to water ...

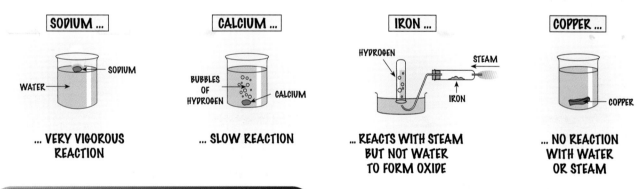

... VERY VIGOROUS REACTION   ... SLOW REACTION   ... REACTS WITH STEAM BUT NOT WATER TO FORM OXIDE   ... NO REACTION WITH WATER OR STEAM

Reaction Of Metals With Dilute Acids

• Metals which react with DILUTE ACID form a METAL 'SALT' and HYDROGEN. A 'SALT' is a word used to describe ANY METAL COMPOUND made when a reaction takes place between a metal and an acid.

$$METAL + ACID \longrightarrow SALT + HYDROGEN$$

• However some metals react more vigorously than others. If we were to add four different metals to acid ...

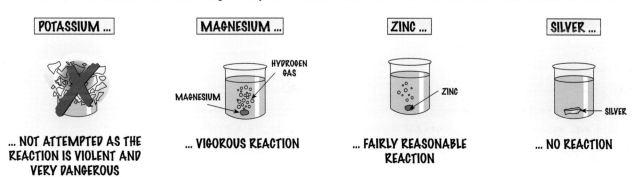

... NOT ATTEMPTED AS THE REACTION IS VIOLENT AND VERY DANGEROUS   ... VIGOROUS REACTION   ... FAIRLY REASONABLE REACTION   ... NO REACTION

THE REACTIVITY SERIES

The REACTIVITY SERIES places metals in order of their reactivity based on how vigorously they react with ...

... ❶ OXYGEN (or AIR)

... ❷ WATER

... ❸ DILUTE ACID

The more vigorously a metal reacts, the higher up the reactivity series it is.

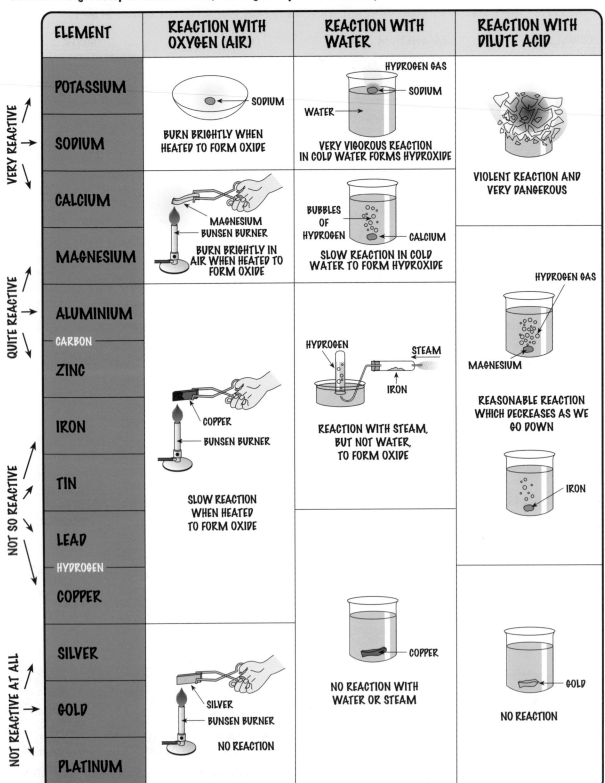

Carbon and hydrogen, although non-metals, are often shown in the Reactivity Series because they can displace less reactive metals from their oxides (See P.22).

A DISPLACEMENT REACTION is one in which a MORE REACTIVE METAL DISPLACES a LESS REACTIVE METAL from a compound. In other words a metal higher up in the Reactivity Series will 'push out' a metal lower in the Series.

- If we put an IRON nail into a beaker of COPPER SULPHATE solution ...

... then a DISPLACEMENT REACTION OCCURS because IRON is higher ...
... in the REACTIVITY SERIES than COPPER.

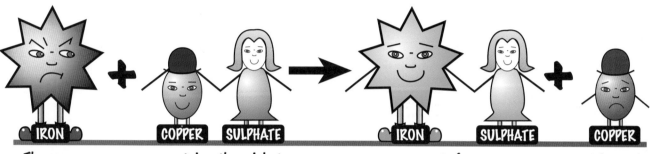

| The more REACTIVE iron ... | ... takes the sulphate from the copper ... | ... to form iron sulphate ... | ... and copper. |

IRON + COPPER SULPHATE → IRON SULPHATE + COPPER

There is one simple rule to remember:

> A METAL HIGHER UP THE REACTIVITY SERIES (MORE REACTIVE) WILL DISPLACE
> A LESS REACTIVE METAL FROM ITS COMPOUND.

Similarly if a mixture of aluminium powder and iron oxide is heated, an extremely vigorous displacement reaction occurs, because ...

MAGNESIUM RIBBON 'FUSE'

ALUMINIUM POWDER AND IRON OXIDE

SMALL PLUG OF IRON REMAINS

... aluminium is higher in the reactivity series than iron.

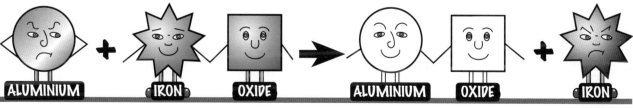

| The more REACTIVE aluminium ... | ... takes the oxygen from the iron ... | ... to form aluminium oxide ... | ... and iron. |

ALUMINIUM + IRON OXIDE → ALUMINIUM OXIDE + IRON

POTASSIUM
SODIUM
CALCIUM
MAGNESIUM
ALUMINIUM
CARBON
ZINC
IRON
TIN
LEAD
HYDROGEN
COPPER
SILVER
GOLD
PLATINUM

Example No. 1   ZINC + COPPER SULPHATE SOLUTION

ZINC + COPPER SULPHATE ⟶ ZINC SULPHATE + COPPER
Yes! Zinc is higher in the Reactivity Series so it displaces the copper forming zinc sulphate.

POTASSIUM
SODIUM
CALCIUM
MAGNESIUM
ALUMINIUM
CARBON
ZINC
IRON
TIN
LEAD
HYDROGEN
COPPER
SILVER
GOLD
PLATINUM

Example No. 2   COPPER + LEAD NITRATE SOLUTION

COPPER + LEAD NITRATE ⟶ LEAD NITRATE + COPPER
No! Copper is lower in the 'series' than lead so no reaction takes place.

Example No. 3   MAGNESIUM + COPPER SULPHATE SOLUTION

MAGNESIUM + COPPER SULPHATE ⟶ MAGNESIUM SULPHATE + COPPER
Yes! Magnesium is higher in the 'series' so it displaces the copper forming magnesium sulphate.

POTASSIUM
SODIUM
CALCIUM
MAGNESIUM
ALUMINIUM
CARBON
ZINC
IRON
TIN
LEAD
HYDROGEN
COPPER
SILVER
GOLD
PLATINUM

POTASSIUM
SODIUM
CALCIUM
MAGNESIUM
ALUMINIUM
CARBON
ZINC
IRON
TIN
LEAD
HYDROGEN
COPPER
SILVER
GOLD
PLATINUM

Example No. 4   SILVER + IRON SULPHATE SOLUTION

SILVER + IRON SULPHATE ⟶ IRON SULPHATE + SILVER
No! Silver is lower in the 'series' than iron so no reaction takes place.

Displacement Reactions Involving Carbon And Hydrogen

Although they are non-metals, carbon and hydrogen often appear in the Reactivity Series because of their ability to displace less reactive METALS from their OXIDES (See P.20).

Example No. 1   CARBON + LEAD OXIDE

CARBON + LEAD OXIDE ⟶ LEAD + CARBON OXIDE
Yes! Carbon is higher in the 'series' so it displaces the lead.
This reaction needs heat for it to occur.

POTASSIUM
SODIUM
CALCIUM
MAGNESIUM
ALUMINIUM
CARBON
ZINC
IRON
TIN
LEAD
HYDROGEN
COPPER
SILVER
GOLD
PLATINUM

POTASSIUM
SODIUM
CALCIUM
MAGNESIUM
ALUMINIUM
CARBON
ZINC
IRON
TIN
LEAD
HYDROGEN
COPPER
SILVER
GOLD
PLATINUM

Example No. 2   HYDROGEN + COPPER OXIDE

HYDROGEN + COPPER OXIDE ⟶ COPPER + WATER
Yes! Hydrogen is higher in the 'series', so it displaces the copper.
This reaction needs heat for it to occur.

Methods Of Extraction

- The Earth's crust contains many naturally occurring elements and compounds called **MINERALS**.
- A **METAL ORE** is a mineral or mixture of minerals from which economically viable amounts of pure metal can be extracted.
- Most ores contain either **METAL OXIDES** or substances which can be easily changed into a **METAL OXIDE**.
- To extract the metal from a metal oxide the **OXYGEN MUST BE REMOVED**.
- The removal of **OXYGEN** is called **REDUCTION**.
- The **METHOD OF EXTRACTION** depends on the metals' position in the **REACTIVITY SERIES**.

REACTIVITY SERIES	METHOD OF EXTRACTION
POTASSIUM SODIUM CALCIUM MAGNESIUM ALUMINIUM	For metals above carbon energy is required to extract them from their ores because they are very reactive metals. **ELECTROLYSIS** is used.
— CARBON —	
ZINC IRON TIN LEAD COPPER	These metals are below carbon in the reactivity series and are extracted from their ores by heating with carbon/carbon monoxide.
SILVER GOLD PLATINUM	These metals are unreactive and exist **NATURALLY**. They are obtained by physical processes eg. panning.

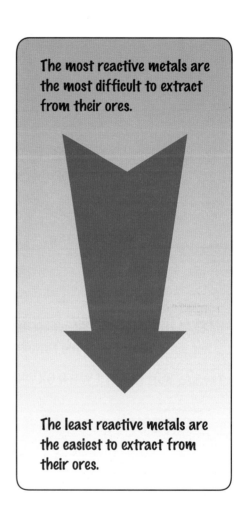

The most reactive metals are the most difficult to extract from their ores.

The least reactive metals are the easiest to extract from their ores.

Corrosion Of Iron

- Iron (or steel) corrodes more quickly than most other transition metals but this can be prevented by connecting the iron to a more reactive metal such as zinc or magnesium.
- The more reactive metal reacts preferentially with the water and oxygen thus preventing it reacting with the iron.
- Zinc bars are attached to the hulls of ships, and magnesium strips to underground steel pipes to prevent corrosion. Only when these have corroded will the iron or steel begin to corrode.
- **GALVANISING** relies on coating iron objects with zinc. Even if they are scratched they still won't corrode until **ALL** the zinc has gone.
- Some objects, such as knives and forks, are made from non-rusting alloys such as **STAINLESS STEEL** which is an alloy containing chromium.

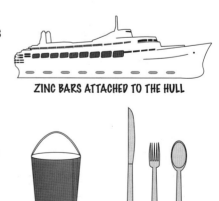

ZINC BARS ATTACHED TO THE HULL

Extraction Of Iron – The Blast Furnace

Iron is BELOW CARBON in the Reactivity Series.
It is one of the most widely used metals in the world: for building, transport and everyday objects.
Haematite is the name of the ore from which iron is extracted.
It contains IRON OXIDE.

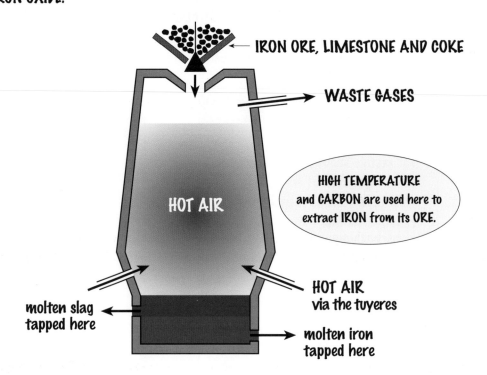

IRON ORE, LIMESTONE AND COKE

WASTE GASES

HIGH TEMPERATURE and CARBON are used here to extract IRON from its ORE.

HOT AIR

molten slag tapped here

HOT AIR via the tuyeres

molten iron tapped here

- HAEMATITE (iron ore), limestone and coke (carbon) are fed into the top of the furnace ...
  ... hot air is blasted in at the bottom.

- The CARBON REACTS WITH OXYGEN to form CARBON DIOXIDE and a great deal of heat energy.

  CARBON   +   OXYGEN ⟶   CARBON DIOXIDE   +   HEAT

- At these high temperatures the CARBON DIOXIDE will react with more carbon to form CARBON MONOXIDE.

  CARBON DIOXIDE   +   CARBON ⟶   CARBON MONOXIDE

- CARBON MONOXIDE IS A REDUCING AGENT and will take the oxygen from the iron oxide leaving just iron.
  ie. it 'reduces' the iron oxide to molten iron which flows to the bottom of the furnace where it can be tapped off. Carbon itself is often used to reduce oxides as it is quite high in the Reactivity Series. However, here it is CARBON MONOXIDE which acts as the REDUCING AGENT.

  IRON OXIDE   +   CARBON MONOXIDE ⟶   IRON   +   CARBON DIOXIDE

This process by which carbon monoxide combines with oxygen from iron oxide to form carbon dioxide is called OXIDATION.

- LIMESTONE is added to remove ACIDIC IMPURITIES forming a MOLTEN SLAG that floats on the surface of the molten iron.

pH Scale And Indicators

When a substance dissolves in water it forms an AQUEOUS solution. The solution may be ACIDIC, ALKALINE or NEUTRAL. Water itself is neutral. The pH scale is a measure of the acidity or alkalinity of an aqueous solution, across a 14 point scale.

VERY ACIDIC				SLIGHTLY ACIDIC		NEUTRAL	SLIGHTLY ALKALINE						VERY ALKALINE
1	2	3	4	5	6	7	8	9	10	11	12	13	14

- When substances dissolve in water, they dissociate into their individual IONS.
- Alkalis contain HYDROXIDE ions. $OH^-_{(aq)}$ • Acids contain HYDROGEN ions. $H^+_{(aq)}$
- INDICATORS, however, are useful dyes that can be used to show by the way their colours change, whether a solution is acidic, alkaline or neutral.

Salts Of Alkali Metals

Compounds of alkali metals, called SALTS which are neutral, can be made by reacting solutions of their hydroxides (which are alkaline) with a particular acid. This is because acids and alkalis are 'chemical opposites' and if they are added together in the correct amounts they can 'cancel' each other out. This is called NEUTRALISATION because the solution which remains has a neutral pH of 7.

ACID + ALKALINE HYDROXIDE SOLUTION ⟶ NEUTRAL SALT SOLUTION + WATER

The particular salt produced depends on the METAL IN THE ALKALI, and the ACID USED, for example ...

POTASSIUM HYDROXIDE + HYDROCHLORIC ACID ⟶ POTASSIUM CHLORIDE + WATER

$$KOH + HCl \longrightarrow KCl + H_2O$$

OTHER EXAMPLES ...	HYDROCHLORIC ACID	SULPHURIC ACID	NITRIC ACID
+ SODIUM HYDROXIDE	→ SODIUM CHLORIDE + WATER	→ SODIUM SULPHATE + WATER	→ SODIUM NITRATE + WATER
+ POTASSIUM HYDROXIDE	→ POTASSIUM CHLORIDE + WATER	→ POTASSIUM SULPHATE + WATER	→ POTASSIUM NITRATE + WATER

Ammonia also dissolves in water to produce an alkaline solution. This can be neutralised with acids to produce ammonium salts.

+ AMMONIA	→ AMMONIUM CHLORIDE	→ AMMONIUM SULPHATE	→ AMMONIUM NITRATE

REMEMBER! THIS RULE ALWAYS APPLIES ...

- HYDROCHLORIC ACID produces CHLORIDE salts.
- SULPHURIC ACID produces SULPHATE salts.
- NITRIC ACID produces NITRATE salts.

All the above reactions can be summarised more simply if we look to what's happening to the hydrogen ions $H^+_{(aq)}$ and the hydroxide ions $OH^-_{(aq)}$ in the acid and alkali.

$$H^+_{(aq)} + OH^-_{(aq)} \longrightarrow H_2O_{(l)}$$

Limestone is a SEDIMENTARY ROCK ...
... which consists mainly of CALCIUM CARBONATE.
It is cheap ...
    ... easy to obtain ...
        ... and has many uses:

1. Neutralising Agent

- Excess ACIDITY of soils can cause crop failure.
    - Alkalis can be 'washed out' by acid rain.
        - Powdered limestone can correct this ...
            - ... but it works quite slowly.
- However, when CALCIUM CARBONATE is heated in a kiln...
... a THERMAL DECOMPOSITION reaction takes place ...
... and the calcium carbonate breaks down into the more ...
... simple substances, CALCIUM OXIDE (QUICKLIME) and carbon dioxide.

NB
Other carbonates behave very similarly when they are heated.

$$\text{CALCIUM CARBONATE} \xrightarrow{\text{HEAT}} \text{CALCIUM OXIDE} + \text{CARBON DIOXIDE}$$
(limestone)   (quicklime)

- This can then be 'SLAKED' with water to produce CALCIUM HYDROXIDE (SLAKED LIME).

$$\text{CALCIUM OXIDE} \xrightarrow{\text{WATER}} \text{CALCIUM HYDROXIDE}$$
(quicklime)   (slaked lime)

- This, being a HYDROXIDE, is quite strongly ALKALINE ...
    - ... and so can neutralise soils and lakes much faster than just using powdered limestone.

2. Building Material

- Can be QUARRIED and cut ...
    - ... into BLOCKS, and used directly ...
        - ... to build WALLS of houses, ...
            - ... in regions where it is plentiful!
                - It is badly affected by ACID RAIN, ...
                    - ... but this takes a long time.

3. Cement Making

CEMENT

- Powdered limestone and powdered CLAY ...
    - ... are roasted in a ROTARY KILN, ...
        - ... to produce dry cement.
            - When the cement is mixed with ...
                - ...WATER, SAND and GRAVEL (crushed rock) ...
                    - ... a slow reaction takes place where ...
                        - ... a HARD, STONE-LIKE BUILDING MATERIAL, ...
                            - ... called CONCRETE, is produced.

Formation Of Crude Oil

- Crude oil, coal and natural gas are FOSSIL FUELS.
- These are fuels which have formed over MILLIONS of years ...
- ... by the action of HEAT and PRESSURE, in the absence of oxygen,
- ... on ORGANIC material from ANIMALS and PLANTS.
- This material gets trapped by layers of sedimentary rock.

Crude oil and natural gas were formed from animals that lived in the sea.

Layers of dead sea creatures formed on the sea bed.

Layers of sedimentary rock formed on top and the creatures became trapped.

After millions of years oil began to form, in the absence of oxygen.

- Natural gas is usually formed with crude oil.

What Crude Oil Is

- Crude oil is a mixture of compounds most of which ...
- ... are MOLECULES made up of CARBON and HYDROGEN atoms only, called HYDROCARBONS.

These hydrocarbon molecules vary in size. This affects their properties.

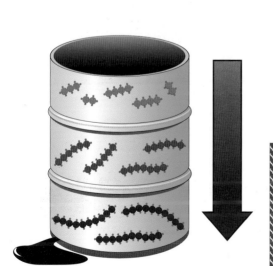

The LARGER the HYDROCARBON
ie. the greater the number of carbon atoms in a molecule:

1 The **LESS VOLATILE IT IS** ...
... ie. it doesn't vaporise as easily.

2 The **HIGHER ITS BOILING POINT.**

3 The **LESS EASILY IT FLOWS** ...
... ie. the more viscous it is.

4 The **LESS EASILY IT IGNITES** ...
... ie. the less flammable it is.

Because a mixture consists of two or more elements or compounds, which aren't chemically combined together, the properties of the substances in the mixture remain unchanged and specific to that substance. This makes it possible to separate the substances in a mixture by physical methods such as DISTILLATION. (See next page)

Fractional Distillation Of Crude Oil

Crude oil on its own isn't a great deal of use. However, different hydrocarbons have different BOILING POINTS which means that they can be separated into their individual parts, or FRACTIONS, by FRACTIONAL DISTILLATION.

EVAPORATE the oil by heating ...
... and then allow it to CONDENSE ...
... at a RANGE OF DIFFERENT TEMPERATURES ...
... where it forms FRACTIONS ...
... each of which contains ...
... hydrocarbon molecules ...
... with a SIMILAR NUMBER ...
... of CARBON ATOMS.
This is done in a ...
... FRACTIONATING COLUMN

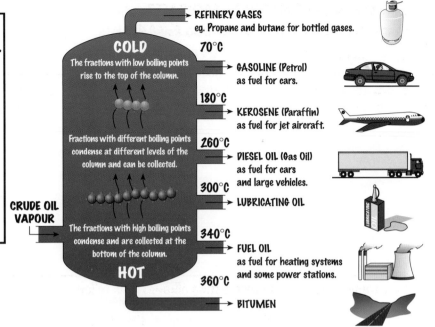

COLD

The fractions with low boiling points rise to the top of the column.

Fractions with different boiling points condense at different levels of the column and can be collected.

CRUDE OIL VAPOUR

The fractions with high boiling points condense and are collected at the bottom of the column.

HOT

→ REFINERY GASES
eg. Propane and butane for bottled gases.
70°C → GASOLINE (Petrol) as fuel for cars.
180°C → KEROSENE (Paraffin) as fuel for jet aircraft.
260°C → DIESEL OIL (Gas Oil) as fuel for cars and large vehicles.
300°C → LUBRICATING OIL
340°C → FUEL OIL as fuel for heating systems and some power stations.
360°C → BITUMEN

Cracking

Because the SHORTER CHAIN HYDROCARBONS release energy more quickly by BURNING, there is a greater demand for them as fuels. Therefore LONGER CHAIN HYDROCARBONS are 'CRACKED' or broken down into shorter chains.

This is done by heating them until they vaporise; the vapour is then passed over a heated catalyst, ...
... where a THERMAL DECOMPOSITION reaction takes place.

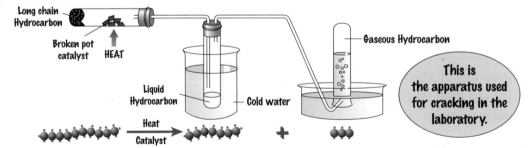

Long chain Hydrocarbon

Broken pot catalyst HEAT

Liquid Hydrocarbon

Cold water

Gaseous Hydrocarbon

This is the apparatus used for cracking in the laboratory.

Heat Catalyst

The products of cracking are used ...

1 ... as FUELS which burn to produce WASTE PRODUCTS, which are then released into the atmosphere. The waste product produced depends on which element is present in the fuel eg.

- CARBON → PRODUCES → CARBON DIOXIDE
- HYDROGEN → PRODUCES → WATER VAPOUR (an oxide of hydrogen)
- SULPHUR → PRODUCES → SULPHUR DIOXIDE

CARBON DIOXIDE   WATER VAPOUR

2 ... to make PLASTICS (POLYMERS) such as POLY(ETHENE) ...

Plastic Bags   Bottles

... and POLY(PROPENE).

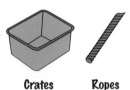

Crates   Ropes

However ...
- Burning fuels does produce carbon dioxide which contributes to the GREENHOUSE EFFECT and sulphur dioxide which helps produce ACID RAIN.
- Most plastics including poly(ethene) and poly(propene) are not BIODEGRADABLE. Microorganisms have no effect on them; they will not decompose and rot away. This causes problems when we throw plastics away as they can build up in landfill sites.

Saturated Hydrocarbons

The 'SPINE' of a HYDROCARBON is made up of a chain of CARBON ATOMS.
- When these are joined together by single covalent carbon—carbon bonds ...
- ... we say the HYDROCARBON is SATURATED.
- Saturated hydrocarbons are known as ALKANES.

To put it simply ...

Hydrogen atoms can make ...
... 1 BOND EACH

Carbon atoms can make ...
... 4 BONDS EACH

The simplest alkane, METHANE, is made up of ...
... 4 HYDROGEN ATOMS and 1 CARBON ATOM.

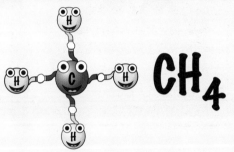

A more convenient way of representing alkanes is as follows ...

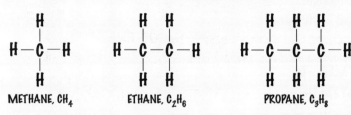

METHANE, CH_4 ETHANE, C_2H_6 PROPANE, C_3H_8

- ALL THE CARBON ATOMS ARE LINKED TO 4 OTHER ATOMS.
- THEY ARE ALL 'FULLY OCCUPIED' OR SATURATED.
- ALL THE BONDS ARE SINGLE COVALENT BONDS.

Because all their bonds are 'occupied' they are fairly UNREACTIVE, although they do burn well.

Unsaturated Hydrocarbons

- Carbon atoms can also form DOUBLE COVALENT BONDS with other atoms, and ...
... amongst the products of cracking are HYDROCARBON MOLECULES which have ...
... at least ONE DOUBLE COVALENT BOND.
We say that the HYDROCARBON is UNSATURATED and it is known as an ALKENE.

The simplest alkene is ETHENE, C_2H_4 which ...

... is made up of 4 HYDROGEN ATOMS ...
... and 2 CARBON ATOMS.
As you can see ethene contains ...
... ONE DOUBLE CARBON = CARBON COVALENT BOND.

Yet again, there is a convenient way of representing alkenes ...

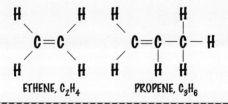

ETHENE, C_2H_4 PROPENE, C_3H_6

- NOT ALL THE CARBON ATOMS ARE LINKED TO 4 OTHER ATOMS.
- THEY ARE NOT ALL 'FULLY OCCUPIED' ie. THEY ARE UNSATURATED.
- A DOUBLE BOND IS PRESENT.

Because of this DOUBLE BOND (=) the ALKENES have the potential to join with other atoms and so they are REACTIVE. This makes them useful for making other molecules, especially POLYMERS.
Polymers are very large molecules which are formed when the small alkene molecules above, called MONOMERS, join together. This process is known as POLYMERISATION.

Monomers To Polymers

One of the important uses of the alkenes which are produced during cracking, is the production of POLYMERS;...
... these are LONG CHAIN MOLECULES, some of which make up PLASTICS.
Because ALKENES are UNSATURATED, they are very good at joining together and when they do so without producing another substance, we call this ADDITION POLYMERISATION.
eg. the formation of poly(ethene) from ethene.

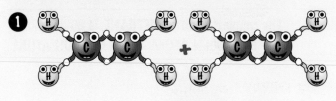

① The small alkene molecules are called MONOMERS.

② Their double bonds are easily broken.

... large numbers of molecules can therefore be joined in this way.

③

The resulting long chain molecule is a POLYMER - in this case POLY(ETHENE) ... often called POLYTHENE

A more convenient form of representing addition polymerisation is ...

ethene monomers (unsaturated)   poly(ethene) polymer (saturated)

General Formula For Addition Polymerisation

This can be applied to any ADDITION POLYMERISATION ...
... to represent the formation of a simple addition polymer.

$$n \left(\begin{array}{c} | \quad | \\ C = C \\ | \quad | \end{array} \right) \longrightarrow \left(\begin{array}{c} | \quad | \\ C - C \\ | \quad | \end{array} \right)_n$$

... where 'n' is a very large number.

For example, if we take ...

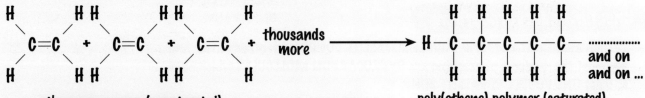

... 'n' molecules of propene to produce poly(propene), which is used to make crates and ropes (see P.28).

Heat (thermal) energy is transferred from HOTTER PLACES TO COOLER PLACES by three different methods, CONDUCTION, CONVECTION and RADIATION.

Conduction

The key point about this type of energy transfer is that the SUBSTANCE ITSELF DOESN'T MOVE. Metals are particularly good conductors while INSULATORS (poor conductors) are also important.

Here is an example of an everyday appliance which uses both a conductor and an insulator.

REMEMBER! CONDUCTION HAPPENS MAINLY IN SOLIDS.

GOOD CONDUCTORS
• ALL METALS especially COPPER and ALUMINIUM
POOR INSULATORS

GOOD INSULATORS
• MOST NON-METALS
• GLASS • WOOD
• PLASTIC
• ALL GASES
POOR CONDUCTORS

Convection

Liquids and gases can FLOW and can therefore transfer HEAT ENERGY from hotter to cooler areas by their own movement (see the diagrams below for the general idea).

Radiation

Energy is continually being transferred to and from all objects by radiation without particles of matter being involved. Hot objects transfer energy through INFRA-RED RADIATION and the hotter the object, the more energy it radiates.

• How much radiation is given out or taken in by an object depends on its SURFACE.

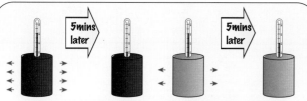

DARK, MATT SURFACES EMIT MORE RADIATION ...
... THAN LIGHT SHINY SURFACES AT THE SAME TEMPERATURE

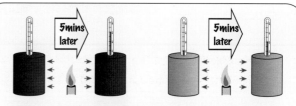

DARK, MATT SURFACES ARE BETTER ABSORBERS (POORER REFLECTORS) ...
... OF RADIATION THAN LIGHT SHINY SURFACES AT THE SAME TEMPERATURE.

Conduction – The Process

Conduction occurs in metals because as the metal becomes hotter its vibrating ions gain more kinetic energy. This energy is transferred to cooler parts of the metal by FREE ELECTRONS as they DIFFUSE through the metal, colliding with ions and other electrons.

POKER

CONDUCTION OF HEAT ENERGY

Convection – The Process

• As the liquid or gas gets hotter, its particles move faster causing it to EXPAND and become LESS DENSE than colder regions.
• The warm liquid or gas will now RISE UP and be replaced by COLDER, DENSER regions.

EXAMPLE A

Candle

EXAMPLE A shows red dye crystals placed in water over a heat source - a CONVECTION CURRENT is set up.
EXAMPLE B shows the circulation of air caused by a radiator - again, a CONVECTION CURRENT is set up.

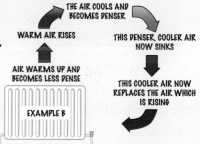

THE AIR COOLS AND BECOMES DENSER
WARM AIR RISES
THIS DENSER, COOLER AIR NOW SINKS
AIR WARMS UP AND BECOMES LESS DENSE
THIS COOLER AIR NOW REPLACES THE AIR WHICH IS RISING
EXAMPLE B

Radiation – The Process

This transfer of energy takes place purely by WAVES - no particles of matter are involved eg. the Sun radiates heat energy to us across the vacuum of space.

Reducing Energy Consumption In Buildings

There are many different ways in which heat losses from a building can be reduced.

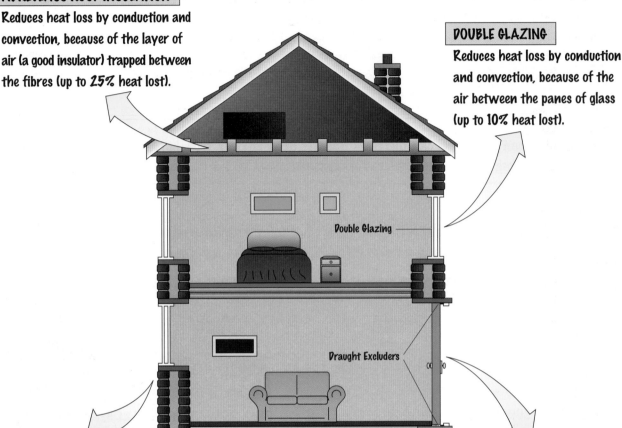

FIBREGLASS ROOF INSULATION
Reduces heat loss by conduction and convection, because of the layer of air (a good insulator) trapped between the fibres (up to **25%** heat lost).

DOUBLE GLAZING
Reduces heat loss by conduction and convection, because of the air between the panes of glass (up to **10%** heat lost).

Double Glazing

Draught Excluders

CAVITY WALL INSULATION
Reduces heat loss by conduction and especially convection by trapping the air in foam (up to **35%** heat lost).

DRAUGHT EXCLUDERS
Reduces heat loss by convection by keeping as much warm air as possible inside (up to **15%** heat lost).

Effectiveness And Cost-effectiveness Of Different Forms Of Insulation

Here is some typical data about the various methods of insulation above:

FORM OF INSULATION	ORIGINAL COST	ANNUAL AMOUNT SAVED	HOW LONG TO PAY FOR ITSELF
Roof Insulation	£400	£80	5 years
Cavity Wall Insulation	£600	£30	20 years
Double Glazing	£1,800	£60	30 years
Draught Excluders	£40	£20	2 years

The most **EFFECTIVE** of these methods is the one which saves the most money each year. In this case the **ROOF INSULATION** with draught excluders being the least effective. However...

... to work out the most **COST-EFFECTIVE** we must consider the issue over a longer period of time, say **4** or **5** years. In this case, we can see that draught excluders have paid for themselves and are now well in profit. Nothing else has, so **DRAUGHT EXCLUDERS** are the most cost-effective.

Most of the Energy transferred in homes and industry is ELECTRICAL ENERGY because it is easily transferred as ...

... HEAT (thermal),   LIGHT ,   SOUND   and MOVEMENT (kinetic) energy.

Power Ratings Of Some Domestic Appliances

Most appliances in the home depend on the transfer of ELECTRICAL ENERGY into other FORMS OF ENERGY. All appliances have a POWER RATING which tells us how much ENERGY IS TRANSFERRED by that appliance EVERY SECOND. The rate of energy transfer is measured in WATTS where 1 watt is the transfer of 1 joule of energy in 1 second.

Here are some examples ...

APPLIANCE				
POWER RATING (W)	120 W	600 W	900 W	2000 W
POWER RATING (kW) 1000 watts (W) = 1 Kilowatt (kW)	0.12 kW	0.6 kW	0.9 kW	2 kW
ENERGY TRANSFERRED PER SECOND (J/s)	120 J/s	600 J/s	900 J/s	2000 J/s

Calculating The Energy Transferred By An Electrical Appliance

The energy transferred by an electrical appliance depends on ...

1 How long the appliance is switched on (in seconds).

2 How fast the appliance transfers energy (its POWER in watts).

It is calculated as follows.

$$\text{ENERGY TRANSFERRED (J)} = \text{POWER (W)} \times \text{TIME (s)}$$

REMEMBER! POWER in WATTS, TIME in SECONDS ——→ ENERGY in JOULES

EXAMPLE

An 1800W electric kettle is switched on for 2 min 30 secs. How much electrical energy will the kettle transfer to heat energy while it is switched on?

Using our formula: ENERGY TRANSFERRED = POWER x TIME

TIME must be in SECONDS remember.

                          = 1800W x 150s

                          = 270,000 joules

The Electricity Meter In Your Home

Your meter at home may show a reading like this ...

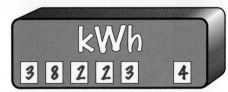

The letters kWh represent ...
... **kilowatt-hours, a unit of ENERGY.**
These are sometimes called 'Units,' and are a measure of the electrical energy you have used.
1kWh = 3,600,000 joules

Your latest bill may look like this ...

REB Regional **Electricity** Board

Meter readings (E=Estimate C=Your Own)

This time	Last time	Units used	Tariff	Pence per unit (kWh)	Amount £
1957	897E	1060	D9	6.5	68.90
Standing charge this quarter					10.00
Total charges this quarter excluding VAT.					78.90
VAT @ 5.0%					3.95
Total Charges this quarter including VAT.					82.85
				BALANCE	£82.85

The Kilowatt-hour

The Kilowatt-hour is a unit of ENERGY ...

... please remember it is NOT a unit of power- that's the kilowatt!!

An electrical appliance transfers 1 kWh of energy if it transfers energy at the rate of 1 kilowatt for one hour.

A 200 watt T.V. set ... transfers 1 kWh of energy if it is switched on for **5 hours.**

A 500 watt vacuum cleaner ... transfers 1 kWh of energy if it is switched on for **2 hours.**

A 1,000 watt electric fire ... transfers 1 kWh of energy if it is switched on for **1 hour.**

Kilowatt-hour Calculations

In order to work out the number of kilowatt-hours or 'Units' transferred by an appliance we need the following formula ...

ENERGY TRANSFERRED (kWh) = **POWER** (kW) x **TIME** (h)

EXAMPLE
A 2000 watt electric hot plate is switched on for 90 minutes. How much does it cost if electricity is 6p per unit?

Using our formula: ENERGY TRANSFERRED = POWER x TIME
= 2 kW x 1.5h
= 3 kilowatt-hours (or UNITS)

But, TOTAL COST = NUMBER OF UNITS x COST PER UNIT

Therefore Total Cost = 3 x 6
= 18 pence

And finally, to do these calculations, you must remember ...
... to make sure the POWER is in KILOWATTS, and ...
... to make sure that the TIME is in HOURS.

THIS PAGE IS FOR STUDENTS STUDYING THE MODULAR SPECIFICATION ONLY.

Gravitational Potential Energy

This is the ENERGY STORED in an object because of the HEIGHT ...
... through which the WEIGHT of the object has been LIFTED ...
... AGAINST the force of GRAVITY.
If an OBJECT CAN FALL ...
... IT'S GOT GRAVITATIONAL POTENTIAL ENERGY.

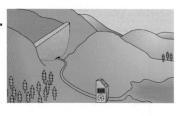

An example of electrical energy being transferred as gravitational potential energy is a ski lift.

Calculating Change In Gravitational Potential Energy

The formula ...

CHANGE IN GRAVITATIONAL POTENTIAL ENERGY (J) = WEIGHT (N) x CHANGE IN VERTICAL HEIGHT (m)

$$\frac{gpe}{mg \times \Delta h}$$

As you can see the formula triangle looks rather nasty, so we'll explain what it means ...

• CHANGE IN GRAVITATIONAL POTENTIAL ENERGY is represented as 'gpe.'

• WEIGHT is represented as 'mg' which is simply the mass, m, of an object multiplied by 'g' which is a constant called the gravitational field strength and has a numerical value of 10 here on earth.

• CHANGE IN VERTICAL HEIGHT is represented as Δh where Δ means 'change in'.

Anyway if you remember them as change in gravitational potential energy, weight and change in vertical height you can't go wrong.

EXAMPLE 1

A skier who weighs 800N takes the ski lift which takes him from a height of 1,000m to a height of 3,000m above ground. By how much does his gravitational potential energy change?
Using our formula:

```
CHANGE IN GRAV. POT. ENERGY  =   WEIGHT  x  CHANGE IN VERTICAL HEIGHT
                             =   800N    x  (3,000m - 1,000m)
                             =   800N    x  2,000m
                             =   1,600,000J
```

... and, as the skier has gone UP, it is an INCREASE IN GRAVITATIONAL POTENTIAL ENERGY.

EXAMPLE 2

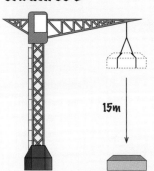

A crane lowers a load of 25,000N from a height of 15m down to the ground. By how much does the gravitational potential energy of the load change?

Using our formula:
```
CHANGE IN GRAV. POT. ENERGY  =  WEIGHT  x  CHANGE IN VERTICAL HEIGHT
                             =  25,000N x  (15m - 0m)
                             =  25,000N x  15m
                             =  375,000J
```

... and, as the load has gone DOWN, it is a DECREASE IN GRAVITATIONAL POTENTIAL ENERGY.

Transfer Of Energy

When devices transfer energy, only part of it is USEFULLY TRANSFERRED to where it is wanted and in the form that it is wanted. The remainder is transferred in some non-useful way and is therefore 'wasted'. Here are four examples of the intended energy transfer and wastage in everyday devices.

1 Tungsten filament light bulb.

ELECTRICAL 100 joules/sec

HEAT 80 joules/sec (wasted)
LIGHT 20 joules/sec (useful)

2 Low energy light bulb.

ELECTRICAL 25 joules/sec

HEAT 5 joules/sec (wasted)
LIGHT 20 joules/sec (useful)

3 Electric kettle.

ELECTRICAL 2000 joules/sec
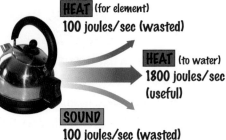
HEAT (for element) 100 joules/sec (wasted)
HEAT (to water) 1800 joules/sec (useful)
SOUND 100 joules/sec (wasted)

4 Electric Motor (a drill includes one).

ELECTRICAL 500 joules/sec

HEAT 100 joules/sec (wasted)
KINETIC 300 joules/sec (useful)
SOUND 100 joules/sec (wasted)

The 'wasted' energy and the 'useful' energy are both eventually transferred to the surroundings which become WARMER.
Unfortunately ...
... this energy becomes so spread out that it becomes difficult for any further useful energy transfers to occur.

Efficiency Of Devices

ELECTRICAL 200 joules/sec
HEAT 150 joules/sec
LIGHT 20 joules/sec
SOUND 30 joules/sec

The greater the proportion of energy supplied to a device, THAT IS USEFULLY TRANSFERRED, the more efficient we say the device is.

For Example ...
... a car engine is 20% efficient - a lot more energy is wasted than is usefully transferred.
... a microwave is 60% efficient - more energy is usefully transferred than is wasted.

Calculating Efficiency

To calculate the efficiency of any device you need to use the following formula.

Remember! A T.V. has both LIGHT and SOUND as useful energy transferred.

$$\text{EFFICIENCY} = \frac{\text{USEFUL ENERGY TRANSFERRED BY DEVICE}}{\text{TOTAL ENERGY SUPPLIED TO DEVICE}}$$

to convert it to a percentage

In the case of the T.V. set shown, ... EFFICIENCY $= \frac{50}{200} \times 100 = 25\%$

Fuels

Fuels are substances which release useful amounts of energy when they burn.
Typical fuels used by humans for generating energy are ...

NON-RENEWABLE FOSSIL FUELS

... COAL   ... OIL   ... GAS   ... WOOD

Coal, oil and gas are energy resources which have formed over millions of years from the remains of living things.
For this reason they are called FOSSIL FUELS, and most of the energy used by humans comes from these sources.

- However, because these energy resources take so long to form, we are using them up at a far faster rate
  than they can be replaced. Hence they are called NON-RENEWABLE ENERGY RESOURCES,
  and will eventually run out.
- **NUCLEAR FUEL** is also a non-renewable, although unlike coal,
  oil and gas it is not a fossil fuel, and is not burnt to release energy.

AN IMPORTANT POINT!

- Wood is NOT a fossil fuel, nor is it non-renewable. It is classed as a renewable energy resource since,
  trees can be grown relatively quickly to replace those which are burnt to provide energy for heating.

Generating Electricity From Non-renewable Energy Resources

The trick in using non-renewables to generate electricity is to ...
... produce heat from the fuel, and use it to make steam which ...
... will eventually turn turbines attached to a generator.

Eg. ❶ Fossil fuels are burnt to release heat energy, ...
    ... which boils water to produce steam, ...
    ... which drives the turbines and ultimately the generators.

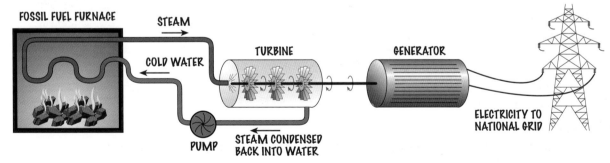

FOSSIL FUEL FURNACE   STEAM   TURBINE   GENERATOR

COLD WATER

ELECTRICITY TO NATIONAL GRID

PUMP   STEAM CONDENSED BACK INTO WATER

Eg. ❷ Electricity is also generated in a similar way ...
    ... using NUCLEAR FUEL
    eg. URANIUM and PLUTONIUM.
    Here a REACTOR is used to generate ...
    ... HEAT and a HEAT EXCHANGER is used ...
    ... to transfer this energy from the reactor ...
    ... to water which turns to steam ...
    to turn the turbines.

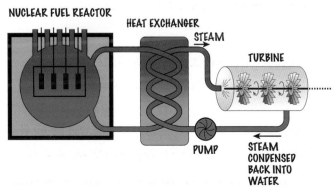

NUCLEAR FUEL REACTOR   HEAT EXCHANGER   STEAM   TURBINE

PUMP   STEAM CONDENSED BACK INTO WATER

- RENEWABLE ENERGY RESOURCES are those that will not run out, because ...
  ... they are continually being replaced.
- This is because many of them are 'powered' by the Sun. For instance, the Sun causes evaporation which results in rain and flowing water, it causes convection currents which result in winds and these winds cause waves.
- Other types of energy resource rely on the gravitational pull of the moon! eg. tides.

Generating Electricity From Renewable Energy Resources

- In renewables, the energy resource is used to drive turbines directly.
  In other words, nothing needs to be burnt to produce heat!

WIND
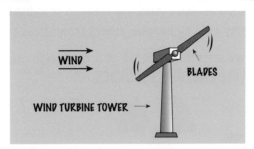

The force of the wind turns the blades of a wind turbine which in turn causes a generator to spin and produce electricity.

TIDAL
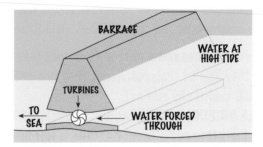

At high tide, water is trapped by a barrage. At low tide the water is released and flows back to the same level as the sea. The movement of this water drives a turbine to generate electricity.

WAVES
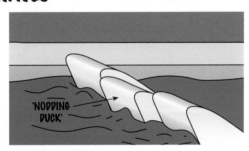

The rocking motion of the waves makes the 'nodding duck' move up and down. This movement is translated into a rotary movement which eventually turns a generator.

HYDRO-ELECTRIC
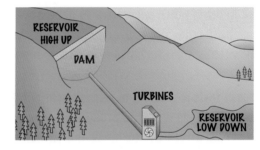

Water stored in reservoirs above the power station is allowed to flow down through pipes to drive the turbines. The water can be pumped back up again when the demand for electricity is low.

GEOTHERMAL

In some volcanic areas, hot water and steam rise naturally to the surface, having been heated up by the decay of radioactive substances (eg. uranium) within the earth. This steam can be used to drive turbines.

SOLAR

Solar cells rely on modern technology to transfer sunlight directly into useful electricity. This has applications in calculators, watches and garden lighting, as well as a more sophisticated use in space probes and satellites.

The four energy sources listed below are used to provide most of the electricity we need in this country directly through power stations. Some of the advantages and disadvantages of each one are listed below ...

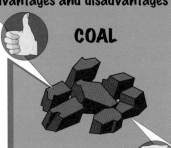

COAL

- Coal is relatively cheap and sometimes easy to obtain.
- Coal fired power stations are flexible in meeting demand and have a quicker start-up time than their nuclear equivalents.
- Estimates suggest that there may be over a century's worth of coal left.

- Burning produces carbon dioxide (CO_2) and sulphur dioxide (SO_2).
- CO_2 causes 'global warming' due to the Greenhouse Effect.
- Coal produces more CO_2 per unit of energy produced than oil or gas.
- SO_2 causes acid rain unless ...
  ... the sulphur is removed before burning ...
  ... or the SO_2 is removed from the waste gases. Both of these add to the cost.

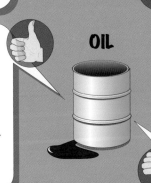

OIL

- There is plenty of oil left in the short to medium term. (30yrs?)
- The price is often variable but it can be relatively easy to find.
- Oil fired Power Stations are flexible in meeting demand and have a quicker start-up time than both nuclear-powered and coal-fired reactors.

- Burning produces carbon dioxide and sulphur dioxide.
- CO_2 causes 'global warming' due to the Greenhouse Effect.
- Oil produces more CO_2 than gas, per unit of energy produced.
- SO_2 causes acid rain (see coal above).
- Oil is often carried between continents on tankers leading to the risk of spillage and pollution.

NATURAL GAS

- There is plenty of natural gas left in the short to medium term. (30 yrs?)
- As relatively easy to find as oil.
- Gas fired power stations are flexible in meeting demand and have a quicker start-up time than nuclear, coal and oil.
- No sulphur dioxide (SO_2) is produced.

- Burning produces carbon dioxide (CO_2) although it is less than both coal and oil, per unit of energy produced.
- CO_2 causes 'global warming' due to the Greenhouse Effect.
- Expensive pipelines and networks are often required to transport it to the point of use.

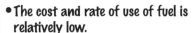

NUCLEAR

- The cost and rate of use of fuel is relatively low.
- They can often be situated in sparsely populated areas (and should be!)
- Nuclear power stations are flexible in meeting demand.
- They <u>don't</u> produce carbon dioxide and sulphur dioxide.

- Although there is very little escape of radioactive material in normal use, radioactive waste can stay dangerously radioactive for thousands of years and safe storage is expensive.
- The cost of building and de-commissioning adds heavily to the unit cost of energy produced.
- They have the longest start-up time compared to coal, oil and gas.

Summary

ADVANTAGES

- Produce huge amounts of energy.
- They are reliable.
- They are flexible in meeting demand.
- They don't take up much space (relatively).

DISADVANTAGES

- They pollute the environment.
- They cause 'global warming' and acid rain.
- They will 'soon' run out.
- Fuels may have to be transported long distances.

You will need to be able to identify and evaluate the financial and environmental costs of using the above energy resources to generate electricity and to evaluate these costs against the benefits to society.

The five energy sources listed below represent the attempts of modern technology to provide us with a clean, safe alternative source of energy. Some of the advantages and disadvantages of each one are listed below ...

WIND

- Wind turbines don't require any fuel and need very little maintenance.
- They don't produce any pollutant gases such as carbon dioxide and sulphur dioxide.
- Once they're built they give 'free' energy when the wind is blowing.

- You need loads of them usually on hills and coastal areas and this can look a bit ugly (visual pollution). Also, noise can be a problem.
- Electricity output depends entirely on the strength of the wind.
- Not very flexible in meeting demand unless the energy is stored.

TIDAL and WAVES

- These devices don't require any fuel.
- They don't produce any pollutant gases such as carbon dioxide and sulphur dioxide.
- Once they're built they provide 'free' energy - at certain times!
- Barrage water can be released when demand for electricity is high.

- Tidal barrages, across estuaries, are unsightly, a hazard to shipping, and destroy the habitats of wading birds etc.
- Output depends on daily variations in the state of the tide and monthly and annual variations in its height, in the case of tidal barrages, and the energy contained in the waves for the 'nodding duck'.

HYDRO-ELECTRIC

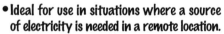

- No fuel is required unless they are operated in reverse to store energy.
- Very fast start-up time to meet sudden increases in demand.
- Large amounts of clean, reliable electricity can be produced.
- When operated in reverse, by pumping water into the higher reservoir, surplus electricity can be stored to help meet future peak demand.

- Location is critical and often involves damming upland valleys which means flooding farms, forests and natural habitats.
- To actually achieve a net output (aside from pumping) there must be adequate rainfall in the region where the reservoir is.

SOLAR

- Ideal for use in situations where a source of electricity is needed in a remote location.
- Excellent energy source when only a small amount of electricity is needed, eg. calculator, watch.
- When in direct sunlight they produce a 'free', clean, although small supply of electricity.

- The amount of electricity produced by solar cells depends on the intensity of light that falls on them. This means they're more useful in sunny places.
- Solar cells have a high cost per unit of electricity produced compared to all other sources except non-rechargeable batteries.

Summary

ADVANTAGES
- No chemical pollution.
- Often low maintenance.
- Don't contribute to 'global warming' and acid rain.
- No fuel costs during operation.

DISADVANTAGES
- Take up lots of space and are unsightly.
- Unreliable (apart form H-E), weather dependent, and can't match demand.
- With the exception of hydro-electric they produce small amounts of electricity.
- High initial capital outlay in building them.

You will need to be able to identify and evaluate the financial and environmental costs of using the above energy resources to generate electricity and to evaluate these costs against the benefits to society.

An ELECTRIC CURRENT is a flow of charge which transfers energy from the battery or power supply ...

... to the components in the circuit. If the component is a resistor, electrical energy is transferred as heat.

An electric current will flow through an ELECTRICAL COMPONENT (or device) ...

... if there is a VOLTAGE or POTENTIAL DIFFERENCE (p.d.) across the ends of the component.

In the following circuits each cell and lamp are identical ...

CIRCUIT 1

Cell provides p.d. ...
... across the lamp.

A current flows and ...
... the lamp lights up.

The amount of current that flows through the component above depends on two things ...

1. The Potential Difference (P.D.) Across The Component

The GREATER the POTENTIAL DIFFERENCE or VOLTAGE across a component ...

... the GREATER the CURRENT that flows through the component.

CIRCUIT 2

Two cells together provide ...
... a bigger p.d. across the lamp.

A bigger current now flows and ...
... the lamp lights up more brightly...
... compared to circuit 1.

2. The Resistance Of The Component

COMPONENTS RESIST the FLOW of CURRENT THROUGH THEM. They have RESISTANCE (measured in ohms).

The GREATER the RESISTANCE of a COMPONENT or COMPONENTS ...

... the SMALLER the CURRENT that ...   **OR**   ... the GREATER the VOLTAGE needed ...
... flows for a PARTICULAR VOLTAGE.   ... to maintain a PARTICULAR CURRENT.

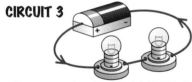 **CIRCUIT 3**   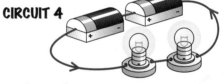 **CIRCUIT 4**

Two lamps together have a GREATER RESISTANCE.   Two cells together provide a GREATER VOLTAGE ...
A smaller current now flows and ...   ... and the same current as in circuit 1 will now flow and ...
... the lamps light up less brightly (compared to circuit 1).   ... the lamps light up more brightly (compared to circuit 3).

Measurement Of Potential Difference And Current

The potential difference (p.d.)
across a component in a circuit
is measured in volts (V)
using a VOLTMETER connected
in PARALLEL across
the component.

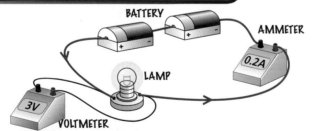

The current flowing through
a component in a circuit
is measured in amperes (A),
using an AMMETER
connected in SERIES.

Standard Symbols For Drawing Circuit Diagrams

The following standard symbols should be known. You may be asked to interpret and/or draw circuits
using the following standard symbols.

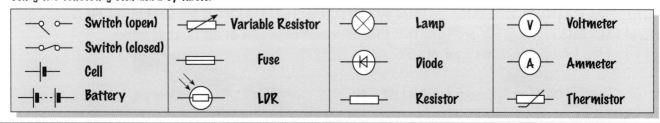

Switch (open)	Variable Resistor	Lamp	Voltmeter
Switch (closed)	Fuse	Diode	Ammeter
Cell			
Battery	LDR	Resistor	Thermistor

Components Connected In Series

In a series circuit, ALL COMPONENTS are connected ONE AFTER THE OTHER in ONE LOOP, going from ONE TERMINAL of the BATTERY to the OTHER. When components are connected in series ...

❶ The same CURRENT flows through each COMPONENT.

ie. $A_1 = A_2 = A_3$

eg. each ammeter reading is 0.1A.

❷ The POTENTIAL DIFFERENCE (p.d.) or VOLTAGE ...
... supplied by the battery is DIVIDED UP ...
... between the TWO COMPONENTS in the circuit.

ie. $V_1 = V_2 + V_3$

However ...
... in our circuit both bulbs have the same resistance and the voltage is ...
... divided equally, but if one bulb had twice the resistance of the other, ...
... then the voltage would be divided differently ie. 2V and 1V.

❸ Each component has a RESISTANCE and ...
... the TOTAL RESISTANCE is the sum of ...
... each individual resistance added together.
eg. if both P and Q each have a resistance of 15 ohms ...
... the total resistance = 15 ohms + 15 ohms = 30 ohms.

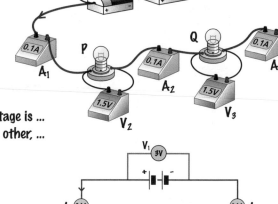

Components Connected In Parallel

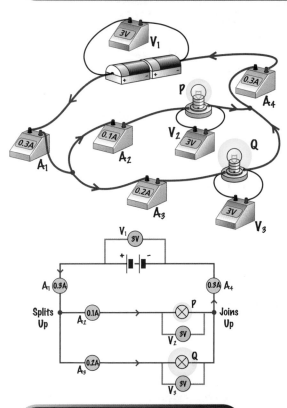

Components connected in parallel are connected SEPARATELY in their OWN LOOP going from ONE TERMINAL of the BATTERY to the OTHER. When components are connected in parallel ...

❶ The TOTAL CURRENT in the main circuit ...
... is equal to the SUM of the CURRENTS ...
... through the separate components.

ie. $A_1 = A_2 + A_3 = A_4$

eg. 0.3A = 0.1A + 0.2A = 0.3A

❷ The POTENTIAL DIFFERENCE ACROSS ...
... EACH COMPONENT is the SAME.
(... and is equal to the p.d. of the battery)

ie. $V_1 = V_2 = V_3$

eg. each bulb has a p.d. of 3V across it.

❸ The AMOUNT OF CURRENT which passes ...
... through EACH COMPONENT depends on the ...
... RESISTANCE OF EACH COMPONENT.
The greater the resistance, the smaller the current.
Bulb P has TWICE the RESISTANCE of bulb Q ...
... and so only 0.1A passes through bulb P ...
... while 0.2A passes through bulb Q.

Connecting Cells In Series

The TOTAL POTENTIAL DIFFERENCE provided by cells CONNECTED in SERIES is the SUM of the P.D. ...
... of EACH CELL SEPARATELY, providing that they have been connected in the same direction.
Each of the following cells has a p.d. of 1.5V ...

Total p.d. = 2 x 1.5V = 3V

Total p.d. = 3 x 1.5V = 4.5V

V = IR

RESISTANCE is a measure of how hard it is to get a CURRENT
through a component at a PARTICULAR POTENTIAL DIFFERENCE or VOLTAGE.
Potential difference, current and resistance are related by the formula:

You are expected to be able to recall this formula.

POTENTIAL DIFFERENCE (volt, V) = CURRENT (ampere, A) x RESISTANCE (ohm, Ω)

Example

Calculate the reading on the voltmeter in the circuit opposite
if the bulb has a resistance of 15 ohms.

$$\frac{V}{I \times R}$$

(we use the letter I for current)

Using our formula: POTENTIAL DIFFERENCE = CURRENT x RESISTANCE

= 0.2A x 15 Ω

= 3V

The reading on the ammeter is the current.

Resistance Of Components

These can be investigated using the circuit above with a power pack instead of batteries.
You could then draw CURRENT-VOLTAGE graphs which show how the CURRENT THROUGH
the component varies with the VOLTAGE ACROSS IT.

❶ RESISTOR

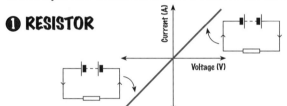

Providing the TEMPERATURE of the RESISTOR ...

... STAYS CONSTANT then ...

... THE CURRENT THROUGH THE RESISTOR IS
DIRECTLY PROPORTIONAL TO THE VOLTAGE
ACROSS THE RESISTOR ...

... ie. if one doubles, the other doubles etc ...

... regardless of which direction the current is flowing.

❷ FILAMENT LAMP

As the TEMPERATURE of the ...

... FILAMENT INCREASES and the ...

... bulb gets brighter then the ...

... RESISTANCE OF THE FILAMENT LAMP INCREASES, ...

... regardless of which direction the current is flowing.

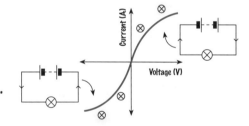

❸ DIODE

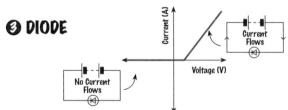

A diode allows a CURRENT to flow through it ...

... in ONE DIRECTION ONLY.

It has a VERY HIGH RESISTANCE ...

... in the REVERSE DIRECTION ...

... and no current flows.

Two Other Components

LIGHT DEPENDENT RESISTOR (LDR)

The resistance of an LDR ...

... depends on the amount of light falling on it.

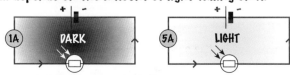

Its RESISTANCE DECREASES as the ...

... AMOUNT OF LIGHT FALLING ON IT INCREASES.

This allows more current to flow.

THERMISTOR

The resistance of a Thermistor ...

... depends on its temperature.

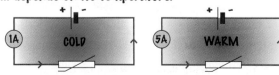

Its RESISTANCE DECREASES as the ...

... TEMPERATURE OF THE THERMISTOR INCREASES.

This allows more current to flow.

Most electrical appliances are connected to the MAINS ELECTRICITY SUPPLY ...

... using a CABLE and a 3-PIN PLUG which is inserted into a SOCKET on the ring main circuit.

In the UK, the mains supply has a VOLTAGE OF ABOUT 230 VOLTS ...

... which if it's not used safely can kill!!

MAINS SUPPLY BY SOCKET

3-PIN PLUG

CABLE

A typical appliance - a kettle

3-Pin Plug

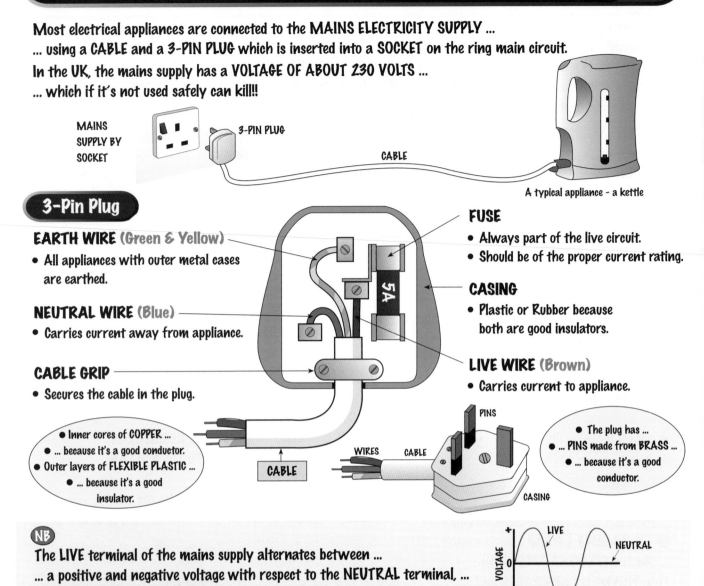

EARTH WIRE (Green & Yellow)
- All appliances with outer metal cases are earthed.

NEUTRAL WIRE (Blue)
- Carries current away from appliance.

CABLE GRIP
- Secures the cable in the plug.

FUSE
- Always part of the live circuit.
- Should be of the proper current rating.

CASING
- Plastic or Rubber because both are good insulators.

LIVE WIRE (Brown)
- Carries current to appliance.

- Inner cores of COPPER ...
- ... because it's a good conductor.
- Outer layers of FLEXIBLE PLASTIC ...
- ... because it's a good insulator.

CABLE

WIRES   CABLE   PINS

- The plug has ...
- ... PINS made from BRASS ...
- ... because it's a good conductor.

CASING

NB

The LIVE terminal of the mains supply alternates between ...

... a positive and negative voltage with respect to the NEUTRAL terminal, ...

... which stays at a voltage close to zero with respect to EARTH.

LIVE   NEUTRAL   VOLTAGE   0   +   −

Errors In Wiring Plugs

It is very important that all plugs are wired correctly with NO errors, for our own safety.

Below are five examples of dangerously wired plugs!

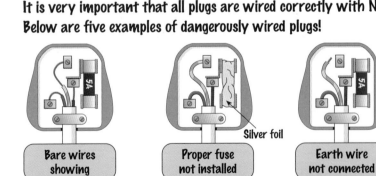

Bare wires showing

Silver foil

Proper fuse not installed

Earth wire not connected

Live and neutral wrong way round

Cable grip loose

Dangerous Practices In The Use Of Mains Electricity

Apart from making sure that all plugs are wired correctly, here are some 'common sense' practices which should be followed at all times:

- All broken plugs and frayed cables should be replaced.
- Keep plugs and cables away from water or heat.
- Never overload a socket with too many plugs.
- Make sure your hands aren't wet when switching appliances on or off.

Alternating Current

This type of current changes direction of flow back and forth continuously. The number of complete cycles of reversal per second is called the FREQUENCY, and for mains electricity this is 50 cycles per second (Hertz). FREQUENCY and VOLTAGE can be compared using an oscilloscope.

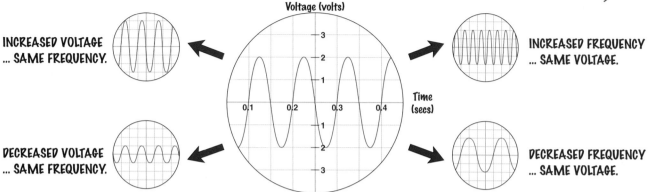

INCREASED VOLTAGE ... SAME FREQUENCY.

INCREASED FREQUENCY ... SAME VOLTAGE.

DECREASED VOLTAGE ... SAME FREQUENCY.

DECREASED FREQUENCY ... SAME VOLTAGE.

In the main example above, the peak voltage is 2 volts and the frequency is 10 cycles per second since one complete cycle takes 0.1 seconds.

Direct Current

This type of current always flows in the same direction. Cells and batteries supply d.c. We can use an oscilloscope to compare the voltage of different d.c. supplies.

Fuses

A FUSE is a SHORT, THIN piece of WIRE with a LOW MELTING POINT.
When the CURRENT passing through it EXCEEDS the CURRENT RATING of the fuse, ...
... the fuse wire gets HOT and MELTS or BREAKS.
This PREVENTS DAMAGE to the CABLE or the APPLIANCE through the possibility of OVERHEATING.

CURRENT LARGER THAN CURRENT RATING OF FUSE → FUSE BURNS OUT → CIRCUIT IS BROKEN → NO CURRENT FLOWS → CABLE OR APPLIANCE IS PROTECTED

However ...
• For this safety system to work properly the CURRENT RATING of the fuse ...
• ... must be JUST ABOVE THE NORMAL WORKING CURRENT of the appliance.

Example Of A Fuse In Action

Normally the current flowing ...
... is **BELOW** the current rating ...
... of the fuse ...
... and the appliance (hairdrier) ...
... works properly.
However ...
... a fault occurs inside the appliance ...

... and the live wire makes contact ...
... with the neutral wire.
The current now flowing is **ABOVE**
... the current rating of the fuse ...
... because there is less resistance.
This causes the fuse wire to get ...
... hotter and hotter until ...

... it gets so hot ...
... it melts!
The circuit is now broken.
No current flows and ...
... there is no danger of ...
... further damage to the appliance ...
... or injury to the user.

Circuit Breakers

Most modern houses tend to have CIRCUIT BREAKERS rather than rely on fuses in the consumer unit.
- They depend on an ELECTROMAGNET which separates a PAIR OF CONTACTS ...
- ... WHEN THE CURRENT BECOMES HIGH ENOUGH.
- They work MORE QUICKLY THAN A FUSE, ...
- ... and are EASILY RESET by pressing a button.

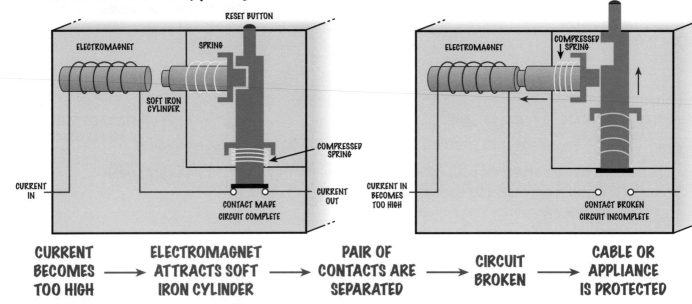

CURRENT BECOMES TOO HIGH → ELECTROMAGNET ATTRACTS SOFT IRON CYLINDER → PAIR OF CONTACTS ARE SEPARATED → CIRCUIT BROKEN → CABLE OR APPLIANCE IS PROTECTED

Many houses though still have consumer units ...
... that rely on ordinary fuses. In these cases, ...
... it is advisable to use an ADAPTER PLUG ...
... which contains a circuit breaker ...
... when using certain appliances ...
... such as a lawnmower or hedge cutter.

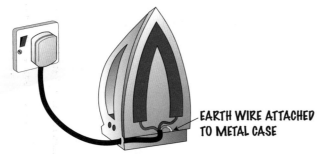

Earthing

All electrical appliances with outer metal cases MUST BE EARTHED.
The outer case of the appliance is connected to the EARTH PIN in the plug through the EARTH WIRE ...

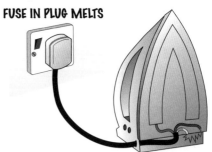

- Normally the current flowing ...
- ... is BELOW the current rating ...
- ... of the fuse.
- The appliance (iron) ...
- ... works properly.

However ...
- ... if a fault in the appliance connects the live wire to the case, then the case will become LIVE!
- This current will 'run to earth' through the earth wire, because this offers less resistance ...
- ... and this OVERLOAD of current will cause the fuse wire to melt (or a circuit breaker to trip).

'LIVE' CASING → SHORT CIRCUIT → CURRENT 'SURGES' TO EARTH → FUSE MELTS → CIRCUIT BROKEN → CABLE OR APPLIANCE IS PROTECTED

Making Electricity By Electromagnetic Induction

- If a wire or a coil of wire cuts through the lines of force of a magnetic field, or vice versa, ...
... then a VOLTAGE IS INDUCED (produced) between the ends of the wire ...
... and a CURRENT will be INDUCED in the wire if it is PART OF A COMPLETE CIRCUIT.

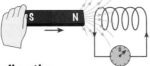

- Moving the magnet INTO the coil ...
- ... induces a current in one direction.

A current can be induced in the opposite direction ...

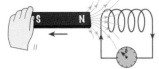

... by moving the magnet out of the coil OR ...

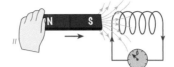

... by moving the other pole of the magnet into the coil.

- Generators use this principle for generating electricity by ...
... ROTATING A COIL OF WIRE WITHIN A MAGNETIC FIELD OR ROTATING A MAGNET INSIDE A COIL.
Both of these involve a magnetic field being cut by a coil of wire, creating an induced voltage.
However, if there is NO movement of magnet or coil there's no induced current.

> In Electromagnetic induction, MOVEMENT PRODUCES CURRENT. This is really the opposite of what happens in the motor effect where CURRENT PRODUCES MOVEMENT.

Increasing The Size Of The Induced Voltage

The size of the induced voltage can be increased if we ...

❶ Increase the SPEED OF MOVEMENT of the magnet or the coil.

❷ Increase the STRENGTH OF THE MAGNETIC FIELD.

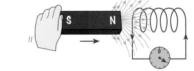

❸ Increase the NUMBER OF TURNS on the coil.

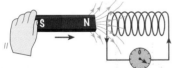

❹ Increase the AREA OF THE COIL.

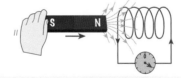

The Alternating Current Generator

Very simply, A COIL OF WIRE IS ROTATED IN A MAGNETIC FIELD, and the same four principles for increasing the size of the induced voltage apply.
As the coil cuts through the magnetic field a current is INDUCED in the coil ...

... which is ALTERNATING ie. it reverses its direction of flow...
... every half turn of the coil, as can be seen below...

Slip Rings

Brush Contacts

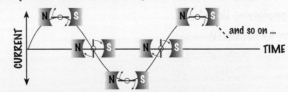

and so on ...

CURRENT / TIME

NB

THE BRUSH CONTACTS are spring-loaded so that they push gently against the SLIP RINGS in order that the circuit remains complete. Gradually they wear away and have to be replaced.

Distributing Electricity

Electricity generated at POWER STATIONS is distributed to homes, schools, shops, factories etc. all over the country by a network of cables called the NATIONAL GRID. Transformers are used to change the voltage of an a.c. supply, and are used both before and after transmission through the grid.

- Before transmission on to the GRID ...
- ...TRANSFORMERS are used to 'STEP-UP'...
- ... the VOLTAGE of the electricity generated.

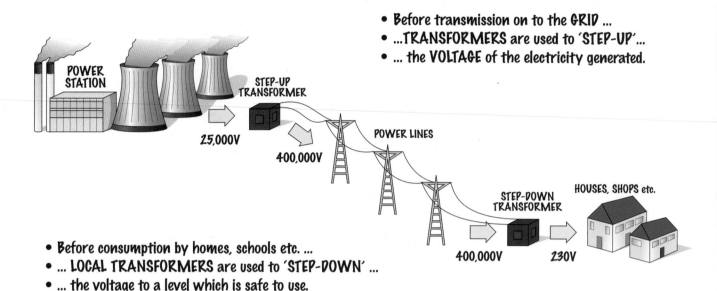

- Before consumption by homes, schools etc. ...
- ... LOCAL TRANSFORMERS are used to 'STEP-DOWN' ...
- ... the voltage to a level which is safe to use.

Reducing The Energy Loss During Transmission

The HIGHER the CURRENT that passes through ANY WIRE ...
... the greater the AMOUNT OF ENERGY LOST AS HEAT FROM THE WIRES.
So we need to transmit as low a current as possible through the POWER LINES.

However, reducing the current means increasing the voltage in order to transmit energy at the same rate and reduce the energy lost as heat.

This is where transformers come in!

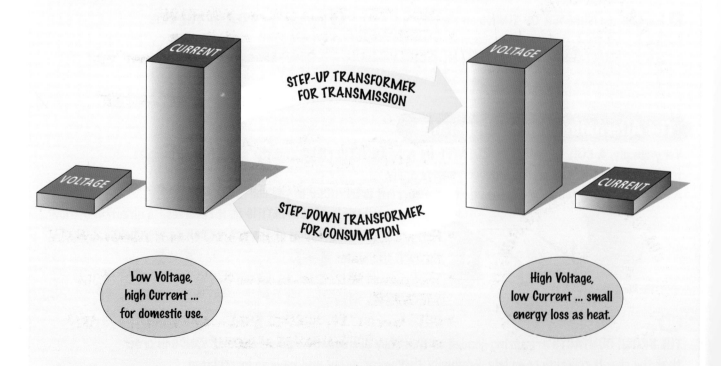

- ADAPTATIONS are SPECIAL FEATURES OR BEHAVIOUR which make an organism...
  ...ESPECIALLY WELL-SUITED TO ITS ENVIRONMENT.

- ADAPTATIONS are part of the EVOLUTIONARY PROCESS which 'shapes life' so that a habitat is populated by organisms which excel there. Adaptations increase an organism's chance of survival; they are 'biological solutions' to an environmental challenge!

Examples Of How Organisms Are Adapted To Their Environment

... LIFE IN A VERY COLD CLIMATE - THE POLAR BEAR

- Rounded shape means a SMALL SURFACE AREA/VOLUME RATIO to REDUCE HEAT LOSS.
- LARGE AMOUNT OF INSULATING FAT beneath the skin, which also acts as a food store.
- THICK GREASY FUR TO ADD TO INSULATION against the cold, and to repel water.
- WHITE COAT so that it is CAMOUFLAGED.
- LARGE FEET to spread its weight on the ice.
- POWERFUL SWIMMER so that it can CATCH ITS FOOD.
- HIBERNATES in the worst weather.

... LIFE IN A VERY HOT CLIMATE - THE CAMEL

- Long, thin legs and neck means a LARGE SURFACE AREA/VOLUME RATIO to INCREASE HEAT LOSS.
- BODY FAT STORED IN HUMP with almost none beneath the skin, means that heat can be lost quickly through the skin.
- SANDY BROWN COAT to CAMOUFLAGE it in the desert.
- LOSES VERY LITTLE WATER through sweating or in urine.
- CAN DRINK UP TO 20 GALLONS OF WATER in one go.

... LIFE IN A VERY HOT CLIMATE - A CACTUS

- No leaves and a compact shape means a SMALL SURFACE AREA/VOLUME RATIO to REDUCE WATER LOSS.
- THICK, WAXY SURFACE to REDUCE WATER LOSS.
- STORES WATER in spongy layer inside its stem.
- SPINES PROTECT THE CACTI from predators who would 'steal' the CACTI'S WATER STORE.
- STOMATA ONLY OPEN AT NIGHT to REDUCE THE AMOUNT OF WATER LOST.
- Some cacti have SHALLOW SPREADING ROOTS ...
  ... to ABSORB SURFACE WATER whilst others have ...
  ... DEEP ROOTS to tap into underground supplies of water.

... LIFE IN AN AQUATIC (WATERY) ENVIRONMENT - THE FISH

- Fish are STREAMLINED in shape to allow them to TRAVEL QUICKLY through the water.
- They possess GILLS that can obtain DISSOLVED OXYGEN FROM THE WATER.
- GILLS have a LARGE SURFACE AREA which INCREASE THE AREA over which OXYGEN CAN BE ABSORBED.

Competition

Organisms compete with each other for ...

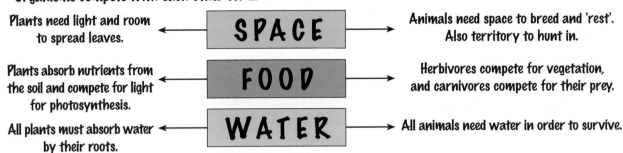

Plants need light and room to spread leaves. → **SPACE** → Animals need space to breed and 'rest'. Also territory to hunt in.

Plants absorb nutrients from the soil and compete for light for photosynthesis. → **FOOD** → Herbivores compete for vegetation, and carnivores compete for their prey.

All plants must absorb water by their roots. → **WATER** → All animals need water in order to survive.

- In addition to competing for the three factors above, animal populations are also affected by PREDATORS, DISEASE and MIGRATION.
- Plant populations are also affected by grazing by HERBIVORES and disease.
- Remember, when we talk about populations here we mean the total number of individuals of the same species which live in a certain area eg. the number of field mice in a meadow. A community is all the organisms in a particular area ie. many populations of plants and animals.

- When two or more organisms compete in a particular area or habitat, the ORGANISMS WHICH ARE BETTER ADAPTED TO THE ENVIRONMENT ARE MORE SUCCESSFUL and usually exist in larger numbers - often resulting in the complete exclusion of the other competing organisms.

In your examination you may be asked to suggest the factors for which organisms are competing in a given habitat.

Predator/Prey Cycles

- Predators are animals that kill and eat other animals while ...
- ... the animals that are eaten are called the prey.
- Within a natural environment there is a delicate balance ...
- ... between the population of the predator and its prey.

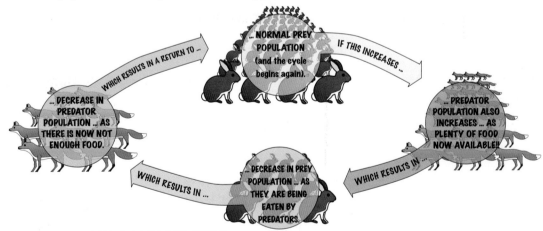

WHICH RESULTS IN A RETURN TO ...

NORMAL PREY POPULATION (and the cycle begins again).

IF THIS INCREASES ...

... DECREASE IN PREDATOR POPULATION ... AS THERE IS NOW NOT ENOUGH FOOD.

... PREDATOR POPULATION ALSO INCREASES ... AS PLENTY OF FOOD NOW AVAILABLE!

WHICH RESULTS IN ...

... DECREASE IN PREY POPULATION ... AS THEY ARE BEING EATEN BY PREDATORS.

WHICH RESULTS IN ...

A classic example - LYNX AND HARES CYCLE

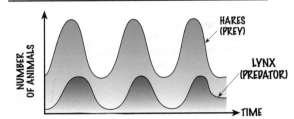

NUMBER OF ANIMALS

HARES (PREY)

LYNX (PREDATOR)

TIME

- Over a period of time the population of ...
- ... lynx and hares does a full cycle.
- There are always more ...
- ... hares than lynx while ...
- ... the population peak for the lynx always comes ...
- ... after the population peak for the hares.

NB THE ABOVE GRAPH WOULD BE VERY SIMILAR FOR **ANY** PREDATOR AND PREY POPULATION CYCLE.

The Population Explosion

The HUMAN POPULATION is INCREASING EXPONENTIALLY, and the standard of living of most people has improved enormously over the past 50 years. This causes the following major problems ...

- Raw materials, including non-renewable energy resources are rapidly being used up.
- Reduction in the amount of land available for other animals and plants (see diagram).
- Increasingly more waste is being produced.
- Improper handling of this waste is leading to an increase in environmental pollution.

HUMAN POPULATION

EXPONENTIAL INCREASE

TIME

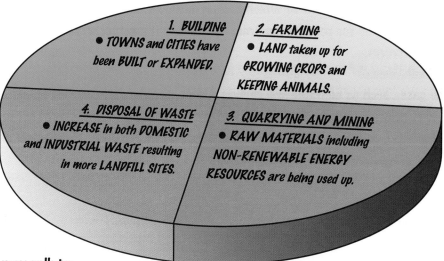

1. BUILDING
- TOWNS and CITIES have been BUILT or EXPANDED.

2. FARMING
- LAND taken up for GROWING CROPS and KEEPING ANIMALS.

4. DISPOSAL OF WASTE
- INCREASE in both DOMESTIC and INDUSTRIAL WASTE resulting in more LANDFILL SITES.

3. QUARRYING AND MINING
- RAW MATERIALS including NON-RENEWABLE ENERGY RESOURCES are being used up.

Pollution

Human activities may pollute:

WATER - with sewage, fertiliser or toxic chemicals.

AIR - with smoke and gases such as carbon dioxide, sulphur dioxide and oxides of nitrogen.

LAND - with toxic chemicals such as pesticides and herbicides, which may be washed from land into water.

- Unless waste is properly handled and stored more pollution will be caused.

Acid Rain

When fossil fuels are burned CARBON DIOXIDE is released into the atmosphere. SULPHUR DIOXIDE and NITROGEN OXIDES are also released from ...

- INDUSTRY • POWER STATIONS • MOTOR VEHICLE EXHAUSTS

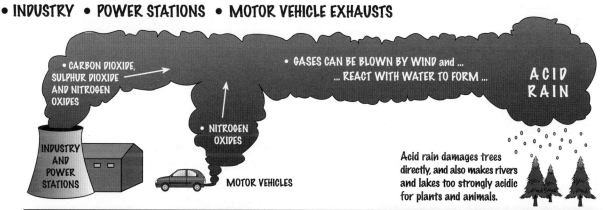

- CARBON DIOXIDE, SULPHUR DIOXIDE AND NITROGEN OXIDES
- GASES CAN BE BLOWN BY WIND and ... ... REACT WITH WATER TO FORM ...
ACID RAIN
- NITROGEN OXIDES
INDUSTRY AND POWER STATIONS
MOTOR VEHICLES

Acid rain damages trees directly, and also makes rivers and lakes too strongly acidic for plants and animals.

Name of waste gas	Effect on Plants and Animals
SULPHUR DIOXIDE	• The gases themselves can HARM PLANTS AND ANIMALS ...
NITROGEN OXIDES (nitrogen oxide and nitrogen dioxide)	• ... but the main problem is the formation of ACID RAIN.

Deforestation

Deforestation involves the large scale cutting down of trees for timber, and to provide land for agricultural use.

This has occurred in many tropical areas with devastating consequences for the environment ...

- Deforestation has increased the release of CO_2 into the atmosphere due to burning of the wood and also as a result of the decay of the wood by microorganisms.
- Deforestation has also reduced the rate at which carbon dioxide is removed from the atmosphere by photosynthesis and locked up for possibly hundreds of years in the actual structure of the wood.

The Greenhouse Effect

This describes how gases, such as methane and carbon dioxide, act like an insulating blanket by preventing a substantial amount of heat energy 'escaping' from the Earth's surface into space. Without any such effect the Earth would be a far colder and quite inhospitable place. However, the levels of these gases are slowly rising and so too is the overall temperature of the planet.

THESE GASES REDUCE THE AMOUNT OF HEAT RADIATED INTO SPACE.

- **DEFORESTATION** - reduces photosynthesis which removes CO_2. Also reduces the rate at which carbon dioxide is 'locked up' as wood.
- **BURNING** - either the chopped-down wood or industrial produces CO_2.
- **INCREASED MICROORGANISM ACTIVITY** - on decaying material produces CO_2.
- **HERDS OF CATTLE** - produce methane, CH_4.
- **RICE FIELDS** - also produce methane.

CAUSE INCREASE IN ATMOSPHERIC CARBON DIOXIDE AND METHANE ...

... WHICH CAUSES GLOBAL WARMING

- Only a few degrees Celsius rise in temperature may lead to ...
    - ... **SUBSTANTIAL CLIMATE CHANGES**, and ...
    - ... a **RISE IN SEA LEVEL.**

What Carbon Dioxide And Methane Do!

In terms of the physics involved, carbon dioxide and methane in the atmosphere absorb lots of the energy that is radiating from the Earth's surface into space. Some of this energy is then re-radiated back to the Earth and so keeps it warmer than it would otherwise be.

CO_2 AND CH_4 ABSORB ENERGY AND RADIATE IT BACK

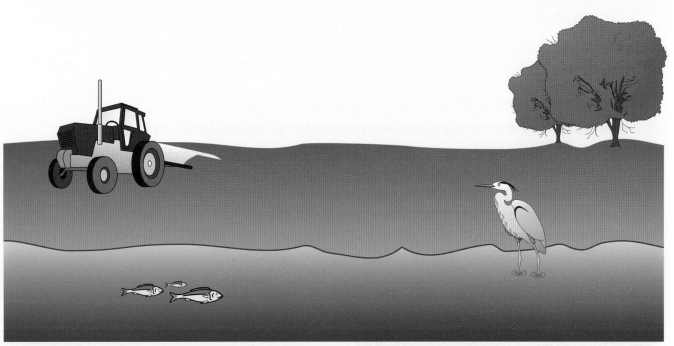

This is the process whereby stretches of water can become stagnant very quickly due to a sequence of events started by carelessness in the overuse of fertiliser.

There are 6 stages:-

1. **INORGANIC FERTILISERS** ... used by farmers may be washed into lakes and rivers. The fertiliser is originally sprayed onto crops to replace the nutrients which previous crops remove.

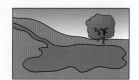

2. **GROWTH** ... of water plants caused by this fertiliser, happens rapidly. The nitrogen in particular is taken up quickly by the plants and used to make protein for growth of new and existing shoots.

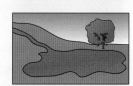

3. **DEATH** ... of some of these plants due to lack of light from over-crowding. The plants literally choke themselves to death as they try to gain sufficient light from the sun, and more nutrients from the water.

4. **MICROORGANISMS** ... which feed on dead organisms now increase massively in number. These are the putrefying bacteria which breakdown dead organic material via respiration, and release simpler substances for recycling.

5. **OXYGEN** ... is used up quickly by this huge number of microorganisms. The process of breakdown is respiration ie. the microorganisms respire the organic material and need oxygen to do so.

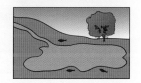

6. **SUFFOCATION** ... of fishes and other aquatic animals due to lack of oxygen in the water. Eventually virtually all the oxygen is removed from the water leaving insufficient for larger organisms.

UNTREATED SEWAGE HAS THE SAME EFFECT AS EXCESS FERTILISER.

- SUSTAINABLE DEVELOPMENT is concerned with three related issues ...
    - ECONOMIC DEVELOPMENT
    - SOCIAL DEVELOPMENT
    - ENVIRONMENTAL PROTECTION

- The UNITED NATIONS EARTH SUMMIT in Rio de Janeiro in 1992 ...
    - ... was arguably the MAJOR EVENT in producing a coordinated WORLDWIDE effort ...
    - ... to produce sustained ECONOMIC and SOCIAL DEVELOPMENT ...
    - ... that would benefit ALL the WORLD'S PEOPLE, particularly the poor ...
    - ... whilst BALANCING the need to protect the environment by REDUCING POLLUTION and ensuring SUSTAINABLE RESOURCES.

- SUSTAINABLE RESOURCES are resources that can be maintained in the LONG TERM at a level that allows APPROPRIATE CONSUMPTION or USE by people ...
    - ... this often requires LIMITING EXPLOITATION by using QUOTAS or ...
    - ... ensuring the resources are REPLENISHED or RESTOCKED.

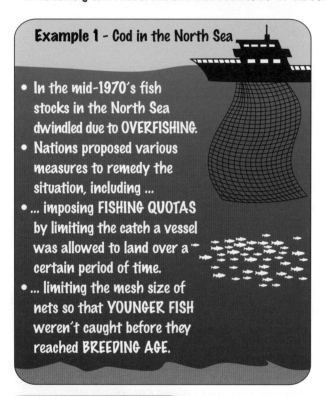

Example 1 - Cod in the North Sea

- In the mid-1970's fish stocks in the North Sea dwindled due to OVERFISHING.
- Nations proposed various measures to remedy the situation, including ...
- ... imposing FISHING QUOTAS by limiting the catch a vessel was allowed to land over a certain period of time.
- ... limiting the mesh size of nets so that YOUNGER FISH weren't caught before they reached BREEDING AGE.

Example 2 - Pine forests in Scandinavia

- Scandinavia uses a lot of pine wood to make furniture, paper and provide energy.
- To ensure the long-term economic viability of pine-related industries ...
- ... companies REPLENISH and RESTOCK THE PINE FORESTS ...
- ... by planting a NEW SAPLING for each mature tree cut down.

Endangered Species

- When COUNTRIES or COMPANIES neglect the ideas of sustainable development ...
    - ... various species can become endangered.

- The RED KITE was exploited ... for its feathers.
- The OSPREY numbers reduced ... as its habitats were destroyed
- The RED SQUIRREL was endangered ... with the introduction of the grey squirrel.

- Many ENDANGERED SPECIES are now PROTECTED ...
    - ... the COUNTRYSIDE COUNCIL FOR WALES provides LEGAL PROTECTION for red squirrels who cannot be trapped, killed or kept except under special licence ...
    - ... the red kite and osprey both have PROTECTED SITES in Wales where they can live and breed undisturbed.
- EDUCATION has become a powerful 'weapon' in ...
    - ... protecting endangered species and promoting the ideas behind sustainable development.

Causes Of Variation

Differences between individuals of the same species is described as VARIATION. Variation may be due to ...

- ... GENETIC CAUSES because of the different genes they have inherited, or ...
- ... ENVIRONMENTAL CAUSES because of the conditions in which they have developed.

However, usually **VARIATION IS DUE TO A COMBINATION OF GENETIC AND ENVIRONMENTAL CAUSES**

An example of some environmental causes ...

IDENTICAL TWINS

An example of some genetic causes ...

The Genetic Information

This information is carried by GENES which are found on CHROMOSOMES.

Different genes control the development of different characteristics.

Many genes have different forms called ALLELES which may produce different characteristics ie. genes for brown eyes and genes for blue eyes are ALLELES; in other words different forms of the same gene!

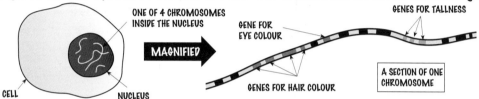

ONE OF 4 CHROMOSOMES INSIDE THE NUCLEUS

GENES FOR TALLNESS

GENE FOR EYE COLOUR

MAGNIFIED

A SECTION OF ONE CHROMOSOME

CELL   NUCLEUS   GENES FOR HAIR COLOUR

Chromosomes come in PAIRS, but different species have different numbers of pairs ...

eg. Humans have 23 pairs. The example above has just 2 pairs!

Mutations

New forms of genes can arise from changes (MUTATIONS) in existing genes.

Mutations occur naturally, but there is an increased risk of mutation if individuals are exposed to MUTAGENIC AGENTS eg. IONISING RADIATION (inc U-V LIGHT, X-RAYS), RADIOACTIVE SUBSTANCES and CERTAIN CHEMICALS. THE GREATER THE DOSE, THE GREATER THE RISK.

Most mutations are HARMFUL and in REPRODUCTIVE CELLS can cause DEATH or ABNORMALITY. In body cells they may cause CANCER. Some mutations are NEUTRAL and in rare cases may INCREASE THE SURVIVAL CHANCES OF AN ORGANISM and its OFFSPRING WHICH INHERIT THE GENE.

Effect Of Reproduction On Variation

SEXUAL REPRODUCTION means LOADS OF VARIATION because genetic information from two parents is 'mixed together' when the male (sperm) and female (egg) gametes fuse!!

The sperm contains 23 chromosomes from the father while the egg contains 23 chromosomes from the mother. The fusion of these two cells produces a ZYGOTE with 23 <u>pairs</u> of chromosomes (or 46 chromosomes). All the body cells produced from this one cell will also contain 46 chromosomes.

(23 pairs actually!)

ASEXUAL REPRODUCTION means NO VARIATION AT ALL because ...

... only one individual is needed as the single parent for it to take place, so ...

... individuals who are genetically identical to the parent (CLONES) are produced.

Bacteria reproducing ASEXUALLY

Mitosis

This occurs for GROWTH and REPAIR (and also in asexual reproduction) and before each cell division a copy of each chromosome is made so that each body cell has exactly the same genetic information.

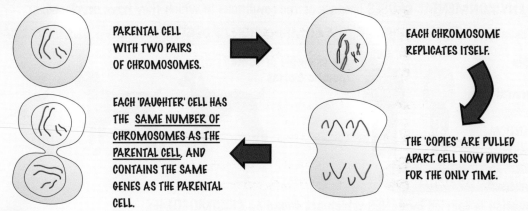

PARENTAL CELL WITH TWO PAIRS OF CHROMOSOMES.

EACH CHROMOSOME REPLICATES ITSELF.

EACH 'DAUGHTER' CELL HAS THE SAME NUMBER OF CHROMOSOMES AS THE PARENTAL CELL, AND CONTAINS THE SAME GENES AS THE PARENTAL CELL.

THE 'COPIES' ARE PULLED APART. CELL NOW DIVIDES FOR THE ONLY TIME.

Meiosis

This occurs in the testes and ovaries to produce the gametes (eggs and sperm) for SEXUAL REPRODUCTION.

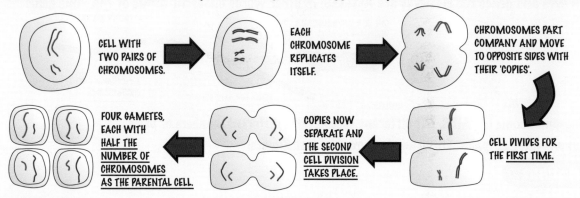

CELL WITH TWO PAIRS OF CHROMOSOMES.

EACH CHROMOSOME REPLICATES ITSELF.

CHROMOSOMES PART COMPANY AND MOVE TO OPPOSITE SIDES WITH THEIR 'COPIES'.

FOUR GAMETES, EACH WITH HALF THE NUMBER OF CHROMOSOMES AS THE PARENTAL CELL.

COPIES NOW SEPARATE AND THE SECOND CELL DIVISION TAKES PLACE.

CELL DIVIDES FOR THE FIRST TIME.

Fertilisation

When gametes join at fertilisation, a single body cell with NEW PAIRS OF CHROMOSOMES is formed. This then divides repeatedly by MITOSIS to form a new individual ...

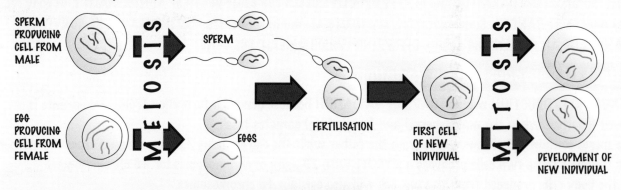

SPERM PRODUCING CELL FROM MALE

SPERM

EGG PRODUCING CELL FROM FEMALE

EGGS

FERTILISATION

FIRST CELL OF NEW INDIVIDUAL

DEVELOPMENT OF NEW INDIVIDUAL

MEIOSIS

MITOSIS

Why Sexual Reproduction Promotes Variation

There are three reasons ...

1. The GAMETES (eggs+sperm) are produced by MEIOSIS, WHICH 'SHUFFLES' THE GENES.

2. Gametes FUSE randomly, with ONE OF EACH PAIR OF ALLELES COMING FROM EACH PARENT.

3. THE ALLELES in a pair may be DIFFERENT (See P.58) and so produce DIFFERENT CHARACTERISTICS.

Inheritance Of Sex – The Sex Chromosomes

- Humans have **23** pairs of CHROMOSOMES, of which one pair are the SEX CHROMOSOMES.

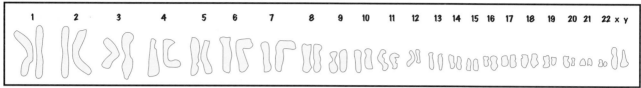

- In females these are IDENTICAL and are called the X chromosomes.
- In males ONE IS MUCH SHORTER THAN THE OTHER and they're called the X and Y chromosomes (Y being the shorter).

THE POSSIBLE PERMUTATIONS

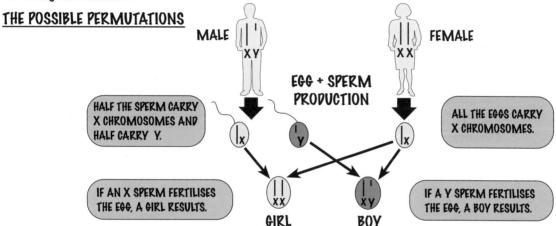

MALE — X Y

FEMALE — X X

EGG + SPERM PRODUCTION

HALF THE SPERM CARRY X CHROMOSOMES AND HALF CARRY Y.

ALL THE EGGS CARRY X CHROMOSOMES.

IF AN X SPERM FERTILISES THE EGG, A GIRL RESULTS.

IF A Y SPERM FERTILISES THE EGG, A BOY RESULTS.

GIRL — XX   BOY — XY

- Like all pairs of chromosomes, the SEX CHROMOSOMES SEPARATE DURING EGG + SPERM PRODUCTION ...
- ... (ie. meiosis) resulting in just one in each sperm or egg.

Ultimately, therefore, the sex of an individual is decided by whether the ovum is fertilised by an X-carrying sperm or a Y-carrying sperm.

Gregor Mendel

- GREGOR MENDEL was born in Austria in 1822 ...
  ... his WORK on PEA PLANTS in 1865 marks the START OF MODERN GENETICS.
- He investigated the HEIGHT OF PEA PLANTS which are all either TALL or DWARF.

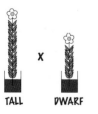

TALL   DWARF

- Mendel started off by taking a plant which was pure-breeding for TALLNESS (ie. when bred with itself or other tall plants they only produced tall plants).
- He then took a plant which was pure breeding for DWARFNESS (ie. it only produced dwarf plants when bred with itself or other dwarf plants).
- He then cross-fertilised these two plants by taking pollen from each one.

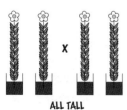

ALL TALL

- To Mendel's surprise ALL the plants produced from the cross were TALL. Mendel based his first law on this which said ...
- 'When pure-breeding plants with contrasting traits are crossed, all the offspring will resemble ONE of the parents'.
- Mendel then crossed several of these tall plants which he had produced.

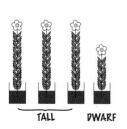

TALL   DWARF

- Again to his surprise he found that there was a 3:1 ratio of tall to dwarf plants. Mendel based his second law on this which said...
- 'For every trait, every individual must have two determiners'.
- We realise now of course that these 'determiners' are GENES but at the time nobody knew about these things. Consequently it was not until 1900 that people recognised the significance of his results.

There are several long words associated with genetics, but don't be put off. The more you use them, the more familiar they will become to you. Here they are ...

ALLELE This is an ALTERNATIVE FORM of a gene. So, for instance, if we were talking about genes for eye colour, we would say that there were two alleles for eye colour, brown and blue. Similarly the genes for being able/not able to roll your tongue are alleles.

DOMINANT This refers to an allele which controls the development of a characteristic when it is present on only one of the chromosomes in a pair.

RECESSIVE This refers to an allele which controls the development of a characteristic only if a dominant allele is not present.

FOR EXAMPLE It's perhaps a little easier to understand if we look at a diagram of a ...
... pair of chromosomes and specifically at genes which code for ...
... eye colour, tongue-rolling ability, and type of ear lobe.

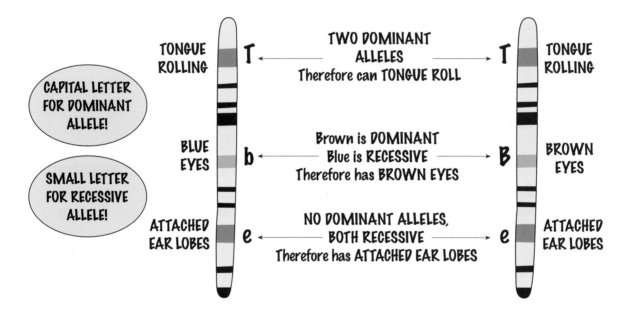

- **DOMINANT ALLELES EXPRESS THEMSELVES IF PRESENT ONLY ONCE ...**
  ... so an individual can be HOMOZYGOUS DOMINANT (BB) or HETEROZYGOUS (Bb) for brown eyes.
- **RECESSIVE ALLELES EXPRESS THEMSELVES ONLY IF PRESENT TWICE ...**
  ... so an individual can only be HOMOZYGOUS RECESSIVE (bb) for blue eyes.

So the possible combinations are ...

	HOMOZYGOUS DOMINANT	HETEROZYGOUS	HOMOZYGOUS RECESSIVE
TONGUE ROLLING	TT (can roll)	Tt (can roll)	tt (can't roll)
EYE COLOUR	BB (brown)	Bb (brown)	bb (blue)
EAR LOBES	EE (free lobes)	Ee (free lobes)	ee (attached lobes)

HOMOZYGOUS If both chromosomes in a pair contain the same allele of a gene then the individual is homozygous for that gene or condition.

HETEROZYGOUS If the chromosomes in a pair contain different alleles of a gene then the individual is heterozygous for that gene or condition.

Monohybrid Inheritance - An Explanation

As we saw on previous pages, genes exist in pairs; one on each of a pair of chromosomes. We call these pairs of genes alleles when they code for alternatives of the same characteristic eg. eye colour. When a characteristic is determined by just one pair of alleles then simple genetic crosses can be performed to investigate the mechanism of inheritance. This type of inheritance is referred to as MONOHYBRID INHERITANCE.

Inheritance Of Eye Colour

In genetic diagrams we use CAPITAL LETTERS FOR DOMINANT ALLELES and LOWER CASE FOR RECESSIVE ALLELES. In eye colour therefore we use B for brown eye alleles and b for blue eye alleles ...

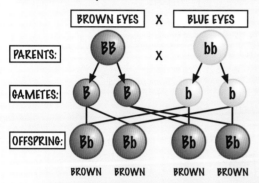
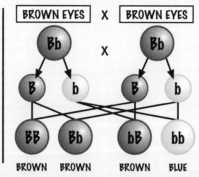
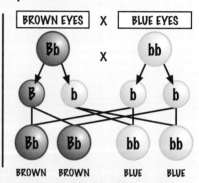

These are the typical examples you may be asked about in your exam. REMEMBER ...
to clearly identify the alleles of the parents ...
to place each of these alleles in a separate gamete ...
and then join each gamete with the two gametes from the OTHER PARENT!!

From the crosses above it can be seen that ...
... if one parent has 2 dominant genes then all the offspring will inherit that characteristic.
... if both parents have 1 recessive gene then this characteristic may appear in the offspring (a 1 in 4 chance).
... if one parent has a recessive gene and the other has 2, then there's a 50% chance of that characteristic appearing. But remember, these are only probabilities. In practice, all that matters is which egg is fertilised by which sperm!

More Advanced Genetics Problems

These usually involve 'wordy' descriptions which you have to translate into crosses.

EXAMPLE 1 Draw genetic diagrams to predict the probable outcome when two heterozygous brown eyed people mate. Brown eyes are dominant to blue eyes.

Ⓐ The genetic diagram reveals a 3:1 ratio of brown eyes to blue eyes.

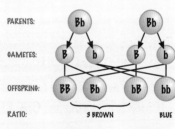

EXAMPLE 2 In mice, white fur is dominant. What type of offspring would you expect to be produced from a cross between a heterozygous individual and one with grey fur? Support your answer with a genetic diagram.

Ⓐ There is a 1:1 ratio of heterozygous individuals to homozygous recessive individuals.

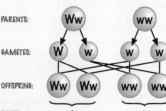

EXAMPLE 3 A homozygous long tailed cat is crossed with a homozygous short tailed cat and produces a litter of 9 long tailed kittens. Show the probable offspring which would be produced if two of these kittens were mated, and describe using genetic terminology the characteristics of the offspring.

Ⓐ The ratio would be 3:1 in favour of long tails. There would be a $1/4$ chance of a homozygous dominant individual, a $2/4$ chance of a heterozygous individual and $1/4$ chance of a homozygous recessive individual.

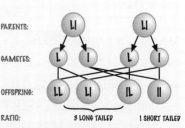

Cystic fibrosis, Huntington's disease and sickle-cell anaemia are three disorders which are inherited.

Cystic Fibrosis – Caused By Recessive Alleles

- Cystic Fibrosis can be passed on by parents, neither of whom have the disorder (ie. they are 'carriers')
- ... if each is carrying just one RECESSIVE allele for the condition.
- It is a disorder of cell membranes causing THICK and STICKY MUCUS ...
- ... especially in the LUNGS, GUT and PANCREAS, which leads to various complications.

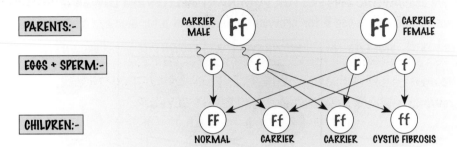

- This particular cross would result in a 1 in 4 chance of producing a sufferer.

Huntington's Disease – Caused By A Dominant Allele

- Huntington's disease, a disorder of the nervous system, is passed on by one parent who has the disorder ...
- ... and therefore is caused by a DOMINANT allele.
- It produces TREMORS, and WRITHING and ultimately can lead to DEMENTIA (loss of sanity).

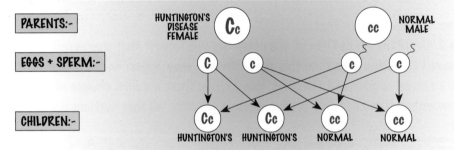

- Here there is a 1 in 2 chance of producing a sufferer.

Sickle-cell Anaemia – Caused By A Recessive Allele

- Sickle-cell anaemia can be passed on by parents neither of whom has the disorder ...
- ... if each is carrying just ONE RECESSIVE ALLELE for the condition.
- Sufferers produce abnormally-shaped red blood cells (SICKLE-SHAPED!), which reduce the oxygen carrying capacity, ...
- ... and they experience general weakness and ANAEMIA.

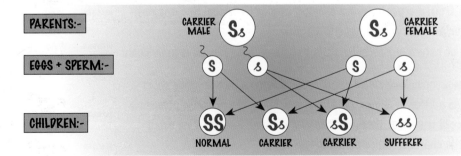

- The HETEROZYGOUS (Ss) INDIVIDUALS also show up to 50% sickling of cells ...
- ... but show an INCREASED RESISTANCE TO MALARIA which is an advantage ...
- ... in areas where MALARIA is prevalent.

Reproducing Plants Artificially

- Plants can reproduce ASEXUALLY ie. without a partner and many do so naturally.
- All the offspring produced ASEXUALLY are CLONES ...
- ... ie. they are GENETICALLY IDENTICAL TO THE PARENT PLANT.

eg. SPIDER PLANT

STOLON - a rooting side branch

NEW INDIVIDUAL ESTABLISHED

NOW INDEPENDENT

TAKING CUTTINGS:

- When a gardener has a plant with all the DESIRED CHARACTERISTICS ...
- ... he may choose to produce lots of them by taking STEM, LEAF or ROOT CUTTINGS ...
- These should be grown in a DAMP ATMOSPHERE until ROOTS DEVELOP.

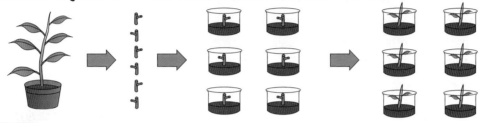

Cloning

CLONES are GENETICALLY IDENTICAL INDIVIDUALS eg. identical twins. So if you've got an organism which is just ideal why not clone thousands of them? This is exactly what's happening in modern agriculture, and this is how ...

<u>1. Taking cuttings</u> ... This is dealt with above.

<u>2. Tissue culture</u> ...

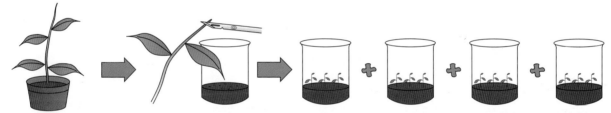

PARENT PLANT - with the characteristics that you want.

A few cells are scraped off into several beakers containing NUTRIENTS AND HORMONES.

A week or two later we've got lots and lots of genetically identical plantlets growing. And we can do the same to these ...

- This whole process must be ASEPTIC (carried out in the ABSENCE OF HARMFUL BACTERIA) ...
  ... otherwise the new plants will ROT.

<u>3. Embryo transplants</u> ... Instead of waiting for normal breeding cycles farmers can obtain many more offspring by using their best animals to produce embryos which can be inserted into 'mother' animals.

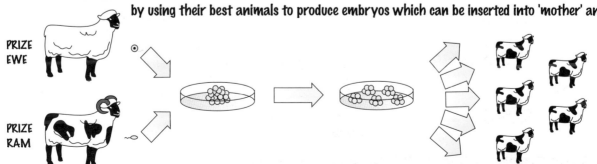

PRIZE EWE

PRIZE RAM

PARENTS with desired characteristics are mated.

Embryo is removed before the cells become specialised ...

... then split apart into several clumps.

These embryos are then implanted into the uteruses of sheep who will eventually give birth to clones.

Selective Breeding Down The Ages

Farmers and livestock have been using the principles of selective breeding for hundreds of years without really understanding the genetic basis for it. The simple rule was to keep the best examples of your animals and plants for breeding and to take the rest to market. The same is true of dog breeders who have systematically selected animals which show the desired characteristics and bred them ...

Choose the two spottiest to breed ...and then the spottiest of their offspring ...   to eventually get Dalmations.

Development Of Modern Cattle

In a competitive farming industry, cattle need to be highly efficient at their job if the farm is to make money. Efficiency means specialisation. In other words cattle have been carefully bred to fulfil certain criteria. In general, this means cattle are selectively bred for one of the following characteristics ...

- **QUANTITY OF MILK PRODUCED ...**
  Some cattle are milk specialists. They churn the stuff out at a great rate and we're all very happy about that. This is no coincidence. These are the result of years of breeding good milk producers with other good milk producers to end up with the champions we have now.

Friesian

- **QUALITY OF MILK PRODUCED ...**
  The amount of fat in milk is a sign of its quality and some cows, although perhaps not producing the same volume as other cows, produce lovely creamy, high fat milk. Again, this is down to artificial selection.

Jersey

- **BEEF PRODUCTION ...**
  The characteristics of the Hereford and Angus varieties have been selected over the past 200 years. They include hardiness, early maturity, high numbers of offspring, and the swift efficient conversion of grass into meat.

Hereford

SELECTIVE BREEDING PRODUCES NEW VARIETIES OF ORGANISM	•	SELECTIVE BREEDING PRODUCES ANIMALS AND PLANTS WITH INCREASED YIELDS

	ADVANTAGES	DISADVANTAGES
CLONING	• Allows LARGE NUMBERS of organisms with the DESIRED CHARACTERISTICS to be produced. • EFFICIENT PROCESS that can increase the economic performance of farmers and plant growers.	• Cloning results in a REDUCED NUMBER OF ALLELES in the population. • LOSS OF VARIATION which reduces the species' ability to respond to environmental change. • Reduces the number of alleles available for further selective breeding (see below).
SELECTIVE BREEDING	• Produces an organism with THE RIGHT CHARACTERISTICS for a particular function. • In farming and horticulture produces a MORE EFFICIENT and ECONOMICALLY VIABLE process.	• Intensive selection results in a REDUCED NUMBER OF ALLELES in the population. • LOSS OF VARIATION which reduces the species' ability to respond to environmental change. • Reduces the number of alleles available for further selective breeding.

Reasons For Genetic Modification Of Organisms

Altering the genetic make-up of an organism can be done for many reasons ...

- To improve the crop yield eg. to produce larger tomatoes, potatoes, wheat seed-heads, more oil from oilseed rape etc etc etc.
- To improve resistance to pests or herbicides eg. Pyrethrum is an insecticide prepared from chrysanthemum plants. The actual gene for Pyrethrum can be inserted into soya plants to provide 'in-built' protection against insect damage.
- To extend the shelf-life of fast ripening crops such as tomatoes.
- To harness the cell chemistry of an organism so that it produces a substance that you require, eg. production of human insulin.

All these processes involve transferring genetic material from one organism to another. In the case of both animals and plants genes are often transferred at an early stage of their development so that they develop with desired characteristics. These characteristics can then be passed onto the offspring if the organism reproduces asexually or is cloned.

Genetic Engineering – The Process

Human insulin can be produced by genetic engineering. This is a hormone, produced by the pancreas, which helps to control the level of glucose in the blood. Diabetics can't produce enough insulin and often need to inject it.

STEP 1

The gene for insulin production is 'cut out' of a human chromosome using RESTRICTION ENZYMES.

These 'cut' DNA at very specific places enabling scientists to remove the precise piece of DNA they want; in this case the gene for insulin production.

STEP 2

Another restriction enzyme is then used to cut open a ring of bacterial DNA (a plasmid). Other enzymes are then used to insert the piece of human DNA into the plasmid. The repaired plasmid is now ready for step 3.

RING OF BACTERIAL DNA CUT OPEN

HUMAN INSULIN GENE INSERTED INTO BACTERIAL DNA

STEP 3

The plasmid is now reinserted into a bacterium which starts to divide rapidly. As it divides it replicates the plasmid and soon there are millions of them - each with instructions to make insulin.

- When the above process has been completed the bacteria is CULTURED ON A LARGE SCALE ...
- ... and COMMERCIAL QUANTITIES OF INSULIN are then produced.

The Great Genetics Debate

- SCIENTISTS have made GREAT ADVANCES in their understanding of genes and ...
① ... have IDENTIFIED GENES that control certain characteristics.
② ... can determine whether a person's genes may lead to them having an INCREASED RISK of CONTRACTING A PARTICULAR ILLNESS eg. breast cancer.
③ ... may soon be able to 'REMOVE' FAULTY GENES and reduce genetic diseases.

- Some parts of society are CONCERNED that ...
① ... unborn children will be GENETICALLY SCREENED and aborted if their genetic make-up is faulty.
② ... parents may want to artificially DECIDE ON THE GENETIC MAKE-UP of their child.
③ ... some insurance companies may GENETICALLY SCREEN applicants and refuse to insure people who have an increased genetic risk of an illness or disease. This may prevent these people being able to drive or buy homes due to lack of insurance.

The Theory Of Evolution

The THEORY OF EVOLUTION states ...

... that all LIVING THINGS which EXIST TODAY and many more that are now EXTINCT ...

... have EVOLVED from simple life forms, which first developed 3,000,000,000 (billion) years ago.

- EVOLUTION is the SLOW, CONTINUAL CHANGE of organisms over a VERY LONG PERIOD ...
  ... to become BETTER ADAPTED to their environment.
- If the ENVIRONMENT CHANGES, SPECIES MUST CHANGE with it if they are TO SURVIVE.
- Species which AREN'T ADAPTED to their environment will become EXTINCT.
- A SPECIES is defined as a group of organisms which can freely interbreed to produce FERTILE offspring.

The Reasons For Extinction Of Species

INCREASED COMPETITION

 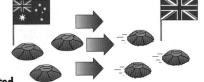

Australian limpets out-competed ...   ... British limpets

CHANGE IN THE ENVIRONMENT

 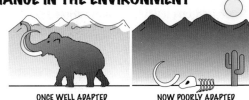

ONCE WELL ADAPTED   NOW POORLY ADAPTED

NEW PREDATORS

The Dodo ... hunted by humans and animals introduced by humans.

NEW DISEASES

The Fossil Record

FOSSILS are the 'REMAINS' of PLANTS OR ANIMALS from many years ago which are found in rock.

Fossils can be formed in various ways ...
- From the hard parts of animals that do not decay easily.
- From parts of animals and plants which have not decayed because one or more of the conditions needed for decay were absent eg. oxygen, moisture, temperature or correct pH.
- Also the soft parts of organisms can be replaced by minerals as they decay. This can preserve the traces of footprints, burrows or rootlets.

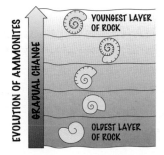

EVOLUTION OF AMMONITES / GRADUAL CHANGE

YOUNGEST LAYER OF ROCK

OLDEST LAYER OF ROCK

- If we look at exposed rock strata, ...
- ... it is possible to follow the GRADUAL CHANGES which have taken place in an organism over time.
- Even though the fossil record is incomplete, these gradual changes confirm that ...
- ... SPECIES HAVE CHANGED OVER LONG PERIODS OF TIME ...
- ... providing STRONG EVIDENCE FOR EVOLUTION.

EVOLUTION BY NATURAL SELECTION

Charles Darwin

He made four very important observations ...
- All living things produce far more offspring than actually survive to adulthood.
- In spite of this, population sizes remain fairly constant, all things being equal.
- There is variation in members of the same species.
- Characteristics can be passed on from one generation to the next.
  From these observations Darwin deduced that all organisms were involved in a struggle for survival in which only the best adapted organisms would survive, reproduce and pass on their characteristics. This formed the basis for his famous theory of 'Evolution by Natural Selection'.
- The reaction, particularly from religious authorities, was hostile to Darwin's theory since they felt he was saying that 'men were descended from monkeys' (which he wasn't) and that he was denying God's role in the creation of man. This meant that his theory was only slowly and reluctantly accepted by many people in spite of the great number of eminent supporters he had.

Evolution By Natural Selection

Evolution is the CHANGE IN A POPULATION over a large number of generations that may result in THE FORMATION OF A NEW SPECIES, the members of which are BETTER ADAPTED TO THEIR ENVIRONMENT.

There are 4 key points to remember:-
1. Individuals within a population show VARIATION (ie. differences due to their genes).
2. There is COMPETITION between individuals for food and mates etc., and also predation and disease. This keeps population sizes constant in spite of the production of many offspring, ie. there is a 'struggle for survival', and many individuals die.
3. Individuals which are BETTER ADAPTED to the environment are more likely to survive, breed successfully and produce offspring. This is termed 'SURVIVAL OF THE FITTEST'.
4. These 'survivors' will therefore PASS ON THEIR GENES to these offspring resulting in an improved organism being evolved through NATURAL SELECTION.

VARIATION and COMPETITION ensure BETTER ADAPTED organisms PASS ON THEIR GENES

Penicillin-resistant Bacteria

This is an increasing problem and is caused by a mutation in the bacteria which confers resistance to penicillin. Consequently non-resistant bacteria are killed off leaving the field free for the resistant ones to reproduce passing on their resistance. This is why doctors are reluctant to prescribe antibiotics when the patient can do without them.

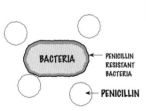

VARIATION	COMPETITION	BEST ADAPTED	PASS ON THEIR GENES
Bacteria MUTATED. Some were resistant to the ANTIBIOTIC PENICILLIN others were not.	The non-resistant bacteria were more likely to be killed by the penicillin.	The PENICILLIN-RESISTANT bacteria survived and reproduced more often.	More bacteria are becoming resistant to penicillin. This is a major health issue.

Conflicting Theories Of Evolution

JEAN BAPTISTE DE LAMARCK (1744-1829) was the first SCIENTIST to try to explain the 'VARIETY OF LIFE'.
- He suggested that an ORGANISM CHANGED to become MORE ADAPTED to its environment.
- For example, a GIRAFFE'S LONG NECK was caused by it STRETCHING TO REACH LEAVES. The longer neck was then passed onto its offspring. Or, that if you kept cutting off the tails of mice for generation after generation they would eventually lose their tails.
- Other scientists believed that God individually created all the different species including those extinct forms found in the fossil record.
- Even now there are many people who do not accept Darwin's theory although it must be said that this is usually based on religious rather than scientific grounds.

Fertility in women can be artificially controlled by giving ...
- ... Hormones that <u>stimulate</u> the release of eggs from the ovaries (FERTILITY DRUGS)
- ... Hormones that <u>prevent</u> the release of eggs from the ovaries (ORAL CONTRACEPTIVE PILLS)

- However, a woman produces hormones naturally that cause the release of an egg from her ovaries, ...
- ... and also cause the changes in the thickness of the lining of her womb.
- These hormones are produced by the PITUITARY GLAND and the OVARIES.

Natural Control Of Fertility ... F.S.H., Oestrogen And L.H.

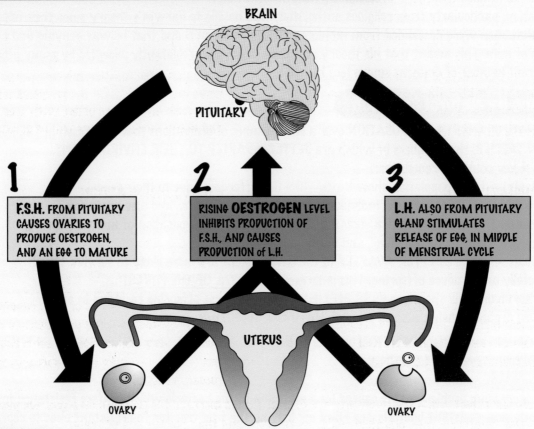

BRAIN

PITUITARY

1 F.S.H. FROM PITUITARY CAUSES OVARIES TO PRODUCE OESTROGEN, AND AN EGG TO MATURE

2 RISING OESTROGEN LEVEL INHIBITS PRODUCTION OF F.S.H., AND CAUSES PRODUCTION of L.H.

3 L.H. ALSO FROM PITUITARY GLAND STIMULATES RELEASE OF EGG, IN MIDDLE OF MENSTRUAL CYCLE

UTERUS

OVARY   OVARY

IN SUMMARY:

HORMONE ...	SOURCE ...	WHAT IT DOES ...
F.S.H.	PITUITARY	CAUSES EGG TO MATURE and OVARIES TO PRODUCE OESTROGEN.
OESTROGEN	OVARIES	INHIBITS PRODUCTION OF F.S.H. and CAUSES PRODUCTION OF L.H.
L.H	PITUITARY	STIMULATES RELEASE OF EGG.

Artificial Control Of Fertility

F.S.H. and OESTROGEN can be given to women in order to achieve opposing results!

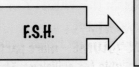

- Given as a FERTILITY DRUG ...
- ... to women who don't produce enough of it ...
- ... to stimulate eggs to mature and be released.

INCREASING FERTILITY

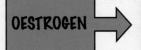

- Given as an ORAL CONTRACEPTIVE ...
- ... to inhibit F.S.H. production ...
- ... so that no eggs mature.

REDUCING FERTILITY

Chemical reactions only occur when **REACTING PARTICLES COLLIDE WITH EACH OTHER** with sufficient energy to react. The minimum amount of energy required to cause this reaction is called the **ACTIVATION ENERGY**. There are FOUR important factors which affect the **RATE OF REACTION**:

TEMPERATURE, CONCENTRATION, SURFACE AREA and USE OF A CATALYST.

Temperature Of The Reactants

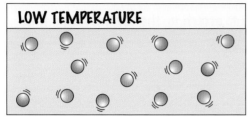

In a COLD reaction mixture the particles are moving quite SLOWLY - the particles will collide with each other less often, with less energy, and less collisions will be successful.

If we HEAT the reaction mixture the particles will move more QUICKLY - the particles will collide with each other more often, with greater energy, and many more collisions will be successful.

Concentration Of The Dissolved Reactants

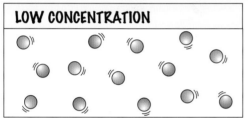
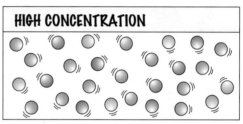

In a reaction where one or both reactants are in LOW concentrations the particles are spread out and will collide with each other less often resulting in fewer successful collisions.

In a reaction where one or both reactants are in HIGH concentrations the particles are crowded close together and will collide with each other more often, resulting in an increased number of successful collisions.

We see a similar effect when the reactants are GASES. As we increase the pressure on a gas, we push the particles closer together - they will then collide more often and the reaction will be faster.

RATE OF REACTION INCREASES

Surface Area Of Solid Reactants

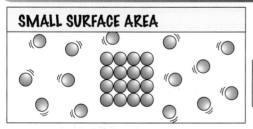

LARGE particles have a SMALL surface area in RELATION TO THEIR VOLUME - less particles are exposed and available for collisions. This means less collisions and a slower reaction.

SMALL particles have a LARGE surface area in RELATION TO THEIR VOLUME - more particles are exposed and available for collisions. This means more collisions and a faster reaction.

REACTION RATE IS SLOW
... where

REACTION RATE IS FASTER

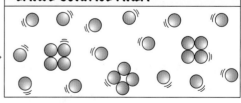

Using A Catalyst

A CATALYST is a substance which INCREASES the RATE of a chemical reaction, without being used up in the process. It can be used over and over again to increase the rate of conversion of reactants into products.

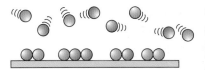

A catalyst lowers the amount of energy needed for a successful collision - so more collisions will be successful and the reaction will be faster. Also it provides a surface for the molecules to attach to, thereby increasing their chances of bumping into each other.

Catalysts are SPECIFIC ie. different reactions need different catalysts ...

eg. • the cracking of hydrocarbons uses BROKEN POTTERY.

• the manufacture of ammonia (Haber process) uses IRON.

Increasing the rates of chemical reactions is important in industry because it helps to reduce costs.

Analysing The Rate Of Reaction

The rate of a chemical reaction can be analysed in TWO ways:

1. Measure the rate at which reactants are used up.

2. Measure the rate at which products are formed.

EXAMPLE ... the decomposition of hydrogen peroxide using manganese (IV) oxide.

HYDROGEN PEROXIDE $\longrightarrow$ WATER + OXYGEN

Measure the mass of the reaction mixture. Oxygen is produced and so the mass of the reaction mixture will <u>decrease</u>.

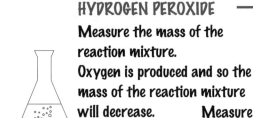

Measure the volume of <u>oxygen produced</u>. A gas syringe can be used.

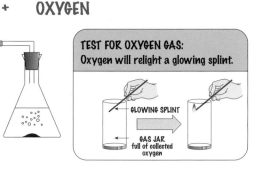

TEST FOR OXYGEN GAS:
Oxygen will relight a glowing splint.

GLOWING SPLINT

GAS JAR full of collected oxygen

GRAPHS can then be plotted to show the progress of a chemical reaction - there are THREE things to remember.

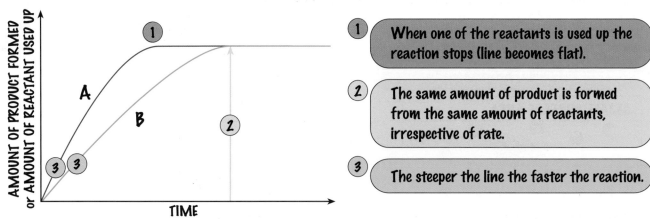

1 When one of the reactants is used up the reaction stops (line becomes flat).

2 The same amount of product is formed from the same amount of reactants, irrespective of rate.

3 The steeper the line the faster the reaction.

REACTION A IS FASTER THAN REACTION B - this could be for one of four reasons:

The SURFACE AREA of the solid reactants in A is GREATER than in B.	The CONCENTRATION of the solution in A is GREATER than in B.
The TEMPERATURE of reaction A is GREATER than reaction B.	A CATALYST is used in reaction A but NOT in reaction B.

ENZYMES are biological catalysts. They are PROTEIN MOLECULES and they control the RATE OF REACTIONS which occur in living organisms. These reactions take place in cells in order to produce new materials.

Biological Detergents

These contain enzymes such as PROTEASES and LIPASES which can digest and therefore remove tough stains from clothes ...
... at LOWER TEMPERATURES than would otherwise be needed.

WASHING POWDER 3KG

Fermentation

Under the right temperature conditions enzymes in YEAST CELLS convert SUGAR into ALCOHOL (ethanol) and CARBON DIOXIDE which is given off in the reaction. This is FERMENTATION and it can easily be demonstrated ...

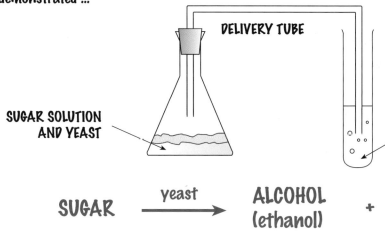

DELIVERY TUBE

SUGAR SOLUTION AND YEAST

A SIMPLE LABORATORY TEST FOR THE CARBON DIOXIDE GIVEN OFF IS THAT IT TURNS LIMEWATER MILKY.

SUGAR →(yeast) ALCOHOL (ethanol) + CARBON DIOXIDE

The ALCOHOL produced during fermentation is used ...
... as the basis for the BREWING and WINE-MAKING INDUSTRIES.

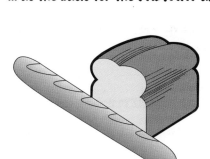

The bubbles of CARBON DIOXIDE produced is used in BAKING ...
... to make the bread rise.

Yoghurt Making

Enzymes in bacteria produce yoghurt from milk ...
... by converting lactose, ...
... a sugar found in milk, to LACTIC ACID ...
... so giving it a slightly sour taste.

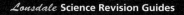

Use Of Enzymes In Industry

In industry enzymes are used to make reactions occur at normal temperatures and pressures that would otherwise require expensive, energy-demanding equipment.

EXAMPLES

1. BABY FOODS

Proteases are sometimes used to 'pre-digest' the protein in some baby foods in order to make them easier to absorb by the infant. Long protein molecules are cleaved into shorter chains of amino acids.

2. CONVERSION OF STARCH TO SUGAR

Carbohydrases can be used to convert starch syrup to sugar syrup so that it can be used as a sweetener in various fillings etc. The sugars produced may be sucrose (as shown in the diagram) or glucose depending on the enzymes used.

3. CONVERSION OF GLUCOSE INTO FRUCTOSE

Glucose and fructose are isomers. This means that they have the same chemical formula but their atoms are arranged in slightly different ways. Glucose can be changed to fructose by isomerase. Fructose is much sweeter and so less is required to sweeten foods. This makes it ideal in slimming foods.

Batch v Continuous Production

- In batch production, the enzyme is mixed with the substrate and left to catalyse the reaction in large reactor vessels. At the end, the product has to be separated from the enzyme, which is expensive, or the enzyme written off and replaced by a new enzyme, which is also expensive.

- In continuous production, the enzyme is IMMOBILISED by attaching it to an inert solid such as resin beads or trapping it inside an alginate gel. This enables the substrate to be constantly poured through the enzyme-immobiliser complex allowing the product molecules to run out free of any enzymes. Obviously since there is no need for separation, this process is cheaper.

SUBSTRATE MOLECULES

ENZYME

RESIN BEAD

PRODUCT MOLECULES

Enzyme 'Shelf-life'

- Because enzymes are protein molecules they are fairly large molecules, consisting of a chain of individual amino acids. Consequently this means that they are fairly delicate and may be easily denatured.

- In order to prevent this, they are stabilised so that unusual pH's or temperatures don't affect them. This usually involves some kind of barrier which prolongs their natural shelf life.

John Dalton

The idea that everything is made up of very small particles is not new! The ancient Greeks were the first to propose such ideas 2500 years ago. Unfortunately they were unable to provide evidence for their ideas and so it was rejected until 1808, when a school teacher, John Dalton, carried out some experiments and re-introduced the idea of these very small particles which he called ATOMS. His theory stated that the atoms of a particular element are all the same, while different elements are made up of different atoms.

Structure Of The Atom

Today we know that all substances are made of atoms. There are about 100 different kinds of atom and each one is made up of even smaller particles ...

The central nucleus is made up of PROTONS and NEUTRONS (with one exception) and is surrounded by ELECTRONS arranged in ENERGY LEVELS (or shells).

This is an atom of fluorine:

The nucleus is surrounded by orbiting electrons ✗ arranged in shells.
A fluorine atom contains 9 electrons.

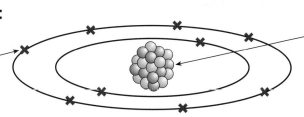

This is the nucleus. It contains protons ⬤ and neutrons ◯. The nucleus is small and heavy. A fluorine atom contains 9 protons and 10 neutrons.

Here are three other atoms ...

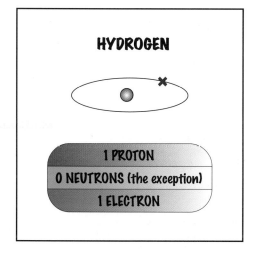

HYDROGEN

1 PROTON
0 NEUTRONS (the exception)
1 ELECTRON

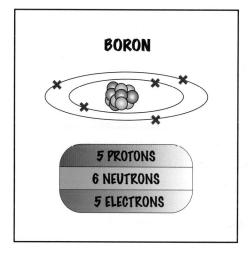

BORON

5 PROTONS
6 NEUTRONS
5 ELECTRONS

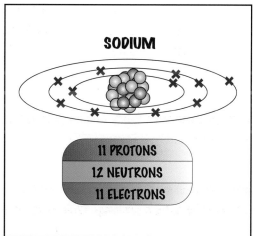

SODIUM

11 PROTONS
12 NEUTRONS
11 ELECTRONS

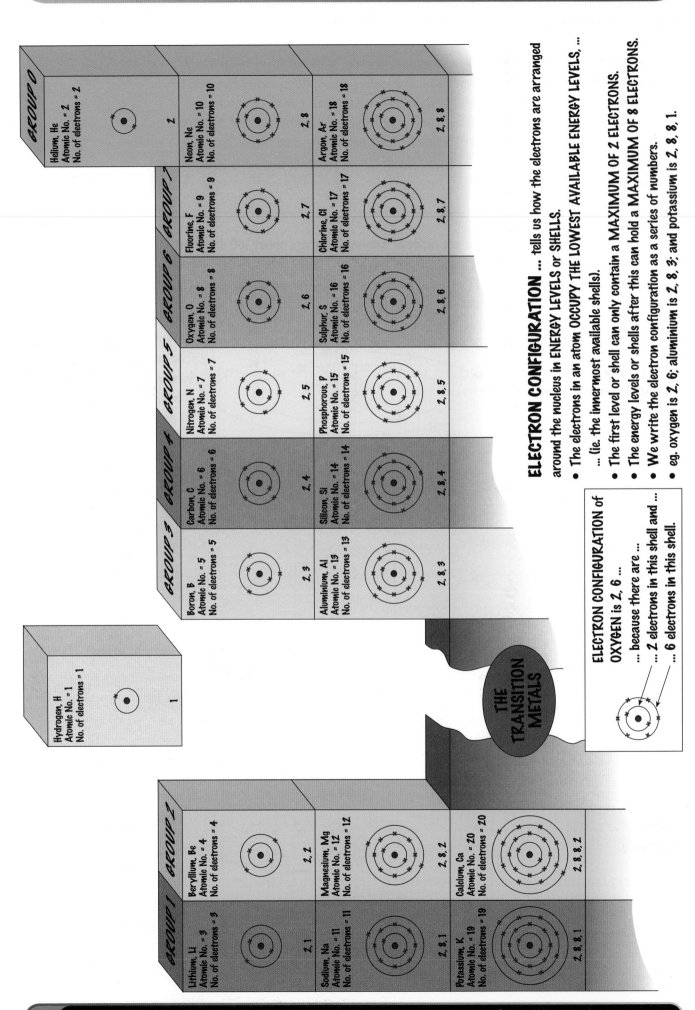

ELECTRON CONFIGURATION ... tells us how the electrons are arranged around the nucleus in ENERGY LEVELS or SHELLS.

- The electrons in an atom OCCUPY THE LOWEST AVAILABLE ENERGY LEVELS, ...
  ... (ie. the innermost available shells).
- The first level or shell can only contain a MAXIMUM of 2 ELECTRONS.
- The energy levels or shells after this can hold a MAXIMUM of 8 ELECTRONS.
- We write the electron configuration as a series of numbers.
- eg. oxygen is 2, 6; aluminium is 2, 8, 3; and potassium is 2, 8, 8, 1.

ELECTRON CONFIGURATION of OXYGEN is 2, 6 ...
... because there are ...
... 2 electrons in this shell and ...
... 6 electrons in this shell.

THE TRANSITION METALS

GROUP 0

Helium, He
Atomic No. = 2
No. of electrons = 2

2

Neon, Ne
Atomic No. = 10
No. of electrons = 10

2, 8

Argon, Ar
Atomic No. = 18
No. of electrons = 18

2, 8, 8

GROUP 7

Fluorine, F
Atomic No. = 9
No. of electrons = 9

2, 7

Chlorine, Cl
Atomic No. = 17
No. of electrons = 17

2, 8, 7

GROUP 6

Oxygen, O
Atomic No. = 8
No. of electrons = 8

2, 6

Sulphur, S
Atomic No. = 16
No. of electrons = 16

2, 8, 6

GROUP 5

Nitrogen, N
Atomic No. = 7
No. of electrons = 7

2, 5

Phosphorous, P
Atomic No. = 15
No. of electrons = 15

2, 8, 5

GROUP 4

Carbon, C
Atomic No. = 6
No. of electrons = 6

2, 4

Silicon, Si
Atomic No. = 14
No. of electrons = 14

2, 8, 4

GROUP 3

Boron, B
Atomic No. = 5
No. of electrons = 5

2, 3

Aluminium, Al
Atomic No. = 13
No. of electrons = 13

2, 8, 3

Hydrogen, H
Atomic No. = 1
No. of electrons = 1

1

GROUP 1

Lithium, Li
Atomic No. = 3
No. of electrons = 3

2, 1

Sodium, Na
Atomic No. = 11
No. of electrons = 11

2, 8, 1

Potassium, K
Atomic No. = 19
No. of electrons = 19

2, 8, 8, 1

GROUP 2

Beryllium, Be
Atomic No. = 4
No. of electrons = 4

2, 2

Magnesium, Mg
Atomic No. = 12
No. of electrons = 12

2, 8, 2

Calcium, Ca
Atomic No. = 20
No. of electrons = 20

2, 8, 8, 2

The Periodic Table

The chemical elements can be arranged in order of their RELATIVE ATOMIC MASSES. The list can then be arranged in rows so that elements with similar properties are in the same columns, or GROUPS.
This forms the basis of the PERIODIC TABLE ...

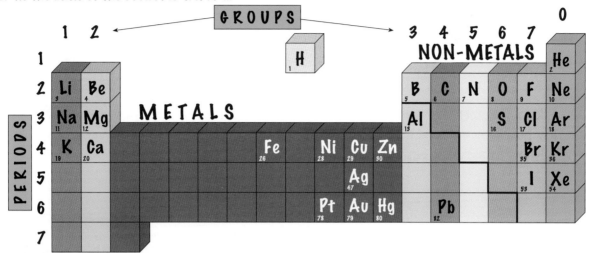

In the modern periodic table, the elements are arranged in order of atomic number since arranging them in order of relative atomic mass results in some oddities such as argon ending up in Group 1 while potassium goes to Group 0!! (instead of the other way round!).

Key Points About The Periodic Table

The periodic table can be seen to be an arrangement of the elements in terms of their electronic structure ...

- ELEMENTS in the SAME GROUP have the SAME NUMBER OF ELECTRONS IN THEIR OUTERMOST SHELL. This number also coincides with the GROUP NUMBER. Elements in the same group have SIMILAR PROPERTIES.
- From left to right, ACROSS EACH PERIOD A PARTICULAR ENERGY LEVEL IS GRADUALLY FILLED WITH ELECTRONS. In the next period, the next energy level is filled etc. (See P.72 for electronic structure).
- Fewer than ¼ of the elements are NON-METALS. They are found in the Groups at the right-hand side of the periodic table.
- The rest are obviously METALS.

Early Attempts To Classify The Elements

JOHN NEWLANDS (1864)

Newlands only knew of the existence of 63 elements. Many were undiscovered. He arranged the known elements in order of RELATIVE ATOMIC MASS and found similarities amongst every eighth element in the series.

This makes sense since the NOBLE GASES (Group 0) weren't discovered until 1894. In other words he noticed PERIODICITY although the 'missing' elements caused problems.

DIMITRI MENDELEEV (1869)

Mendeleev realised that some elements had yet to be discovered, so he left gaps to accommodate their eventual discovery.

He used his periodic table to PREDICT THE EXISTENCE OF OTHER ELEMENTS.

MODERN CHEMISTRY

Although scientists used to regard the periodic table as a curiosity, then as a useful tool, the discovery of ELECTRONIC STRUCTURE gives us a more sound base for the table since the key to similarities amongst elements is the NUMBER OF ELECTRONS IN THE OUTERMOST ENERGY LEVEL ie. Group 1 elements have 1 electron in their outermost energy level, Group 2 elements have 2 electrons and so on.

Group 1 - The Alkali Metals

- The alkali metals all have a low density, ...
  ... the first three being less dense than water, consequently they float.
- Their melting and boiling points decrease as we go down the group.
- Alkali metals react with water to produce HYDROXIDES ...
  ... which dissolve in water to form alkaline solutions, and HYDROGEN.

eg. POTASSIUM + WATER $\longrightarrow$ POTASSIUM HYDROXIDE + HYDROGEN

$$2K_{(s)} \quad + \quad 2H_2O_{(l)} \quad \longrightarrow \quad 2KOH_{(aq)} \quad + \quad H_{2(g)}$$

As we go down the group the alkali metals become MORE REACTIVE and so they react more VIGOROUSLY with water. They float, may melt and the hydrogen gas produced may ignite!! Lithium reacts gently, sodium more aggressively and potassium so aggressively it melts and catches fire.

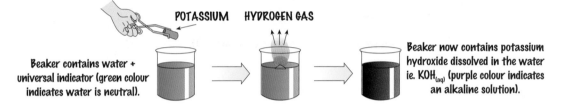

POTASSIUM   HYDROGEN GAS

Beaker contains water + universal indicator (green colour indicates water is neutral).

Beaker now contains potassium hydroxide dissolved in the water ie. $KOH_{(aq)}$ (purple colour indicates an alkaline solution).

A simple laboratory test for the hydrogen gas produced ...
... is that when a test tube of hydrogen is held to a flame ...
... the hydrogen burns with a squeaky explosion (POP!)

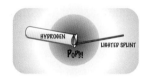

HYDROGEN   LIGHTED SPLINT   POP!!

Group 7 - The Halogens   There are FIVE NON-METALS in this group.

- The halogens have low melting and boiling points, which increase as we go down the group.
- At room temperature fluorine and chlorine are gases and bromine is a liquid.
- They are BRITTLE and CRUMBLY when SOLID ...
- ... and POOR CONDUCTORS of HEAT and ELECTRICITY even when solid or liquid.
- As we go down the group the halogens become LESS REACTIVE.

- A MORE REACTIVE HALOGEN will DISPLACE a LESS REACTIVE HALOGEN from an aqueous solution of its salt ie. chlorine will displace both bromine and iodine while bromine will displace iodine.

eg. POTASSIUM IODIDE + CHLORINE $\longrightarrow$ POTASSIUM CHLORIDE + IODINE

$$2KI_{(aq)} \quad + \quad Cl_{2(g)} \quad \longrightarrow \quad 2KCl_{(aq)} \quad + \quad I_{2(aq)}$$

chlorine gas →

bromine being formed due to the displacement reaction

← potassium bromide solution

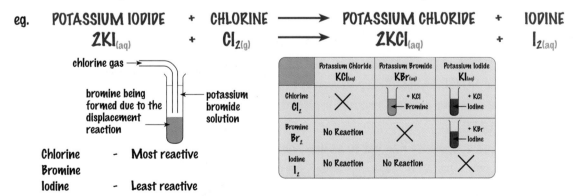

Chlorine   -   Most reactive
Bromine
Iodine   -   Least reactive

	Potassium Chloride $KCl_{(aq)}$	Potassium Bromide $KBr_{(aq)}$	Potassium Iodide $KI_{(aq)}$
Chlorine Cl_2	✕	+ KCl / Bromine	+ KCl / Iodine
Bromine Br_2	No Reaction	✕	+ KBr / Iodine
Iodine I_2	No Reaction	No Reaction	✕

Group 0 - The Noble Gases   There are SIX GASES in this group.

- The noble gases all have low melting and boiling points.
- At room temperature they are all gases.
- They are brittle and crumbly when solid.
- They are poor conductors of heat and electricity (even when solid or liquid).

Trends Within Group 1

They all have ...

... SIMILAR PROPERTIES, because they have ...

... the SAME NUMBER OF ELECTRONS (ONE)

... in their OUTERMOST SHELL, ...

ie. the HIGHEST OCCUPIED ENERGY LEVEL ...

... CONTAINS ONE ELECTRON.

They become ...

... MORE REACTIVE ...

... as we go down the group, because ...

... the OUTERMOST ELECTRON SHELL gets further away ...

... from the influence of the nucleus ...

... and so an electron is MORE EASILY LOST.

 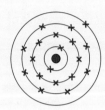

Trends Within Group 7

They all have ...

... SIMILAR PROPERTIES, because they have ...

... the SAME NUMBER OF ELECTRONS (SEVEN) ...

... in their OUTERMOST SHELL ...

ie. the HIGHEST OCCUPIED ENERGY LEVEL ...

... CONTAINS SEVEN ELECTRONS.

They become ...

... LESS REACTIVE ...

... as we go down the group, because ...

... the OUTERMOST ELECTRON SHELL gets further away ...

... from the influence of the nucleus ...

... and so an electron is LESS EASILY GAINED.

Trends Within Group 0

They all have ...

... SIMILAR PROPERTIES, because they have ...

... 'FULLY OCCUPIED' OUTERMOST SHELLS ...

ie. the HIGHEST OCCUPIED ENERGY LEVEL ...

... IS FULL.

Therefore ...

... they don't tend to GAIN ...

.. LOSE or SHARE ELECTRONS ...

... and therefore they are UNREACTIVE ...

... and MONATOMIC.

CHEMICAL REACTIONS

THIS PAGE IS FOR STUDENTS STUDYING THE COORDINATED SPECIFICATION ONLY.

Types Of Chemical Reactions

Below are five different types of chemical reaction. We've included a brief description of each one as well as the relevant page numbers in this guide where further examples can be found.

❶ Thermal Decomposition

In this type of reaction a substance breaks down into simpler substances when heated.

If we take COPPER CARBONATE and heat it ...

... we find that the BLUE/GREEN COPPER CARBONATE decomposes into BLACK COPPER OXIDE and CARBON DIOXIDE.

COPPER CARBONATE ⟶ COPPER OXIDE + CARBON DIOXIDE

Another example of a thermal decomposition reaction is the CRACKING OF LONG CHAIN HYDROCARBONS. (See P.28).

❷ Neutralisation

Acids and alkalis are 'chemical opposites'. If they are added together in the correct amounts they can 'cancel' each other out. This is called NEUTRALISATION because the solution which remains has a neutral pH of 7.

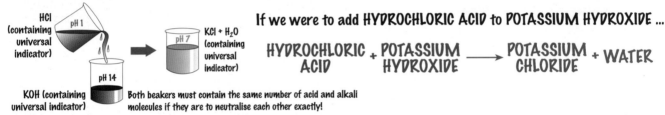

If we were to add HYDROCHLORIC ACID to POTASSIUM HYDROXIDE ...

HYDROCHLORIC ACID + POTASSIUM HYDROXIDE ⟶ POTASSIUM CHLORIDE + WATER

Both beakers must contain the same number of acid and alkali molecules if they are to neutralise each other exactly!

The production of a SALT is an example of a neutralisation reaction (See P.25).

❸ Displacement

This is a reaction in which a MORE REACTIVE METAL DISPLACES a LESS REACTIVE METAL from one of its compounds. (See P. 21 and 22 for examples).

❹ Oxidation

This is a reaction where OXYGEN COMBINES with a substance.
Combustion is an example of an oxidation reaction (See P. 28).
If we burn methane in air (oxygen) ...

METHANE + OXYGEN ⟶ CARBON DIOXIDE + WATER

The extraction of iron using the blast furnace includes some examples of oxidation reactions (See P.24)

❺ Reduction

This is a reaction where OXYGEN is removed from a substance. The extraction of metals from their ores involves the removal of oxygen (See P.23 and 24).

Redox Reactions

In a chemical reaction if OXIDATION occurs ...
... then REDUCTION ALSO OCCURS.
These reactions are called REDOX REACTIONS.
The reaction between iron oxide and carbon monoxide (See P.24) in the extraction of iron using the blast furnace is an example of a redox reaction.

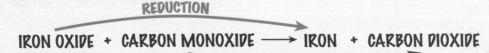

REDUCTION

IRON OXIDE + CARBON MONOXIDE ⟶ IRON + CARBON DIOXIDE

OXIDATION

In the above reaction ...
... the IRON OXIDE is REDUCED to IRON since it loses oxygen while ...
... the CARBON MONOXIDE is OXIDISED to CARBON DIOXIDE since it gains oxygen.

The SOLAR SYSTEM is made up of ...
- ... the SUN which is in the middle ...
- ... surrounded by 9 PLANETS.
- These planets move around the sun in paths called ORBITS ...
- ... which are SLIGHTLY SQUASHED CIRCLES (ELLIPSES).

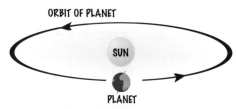

ORBIT OF PLANET

SUN

PLANET

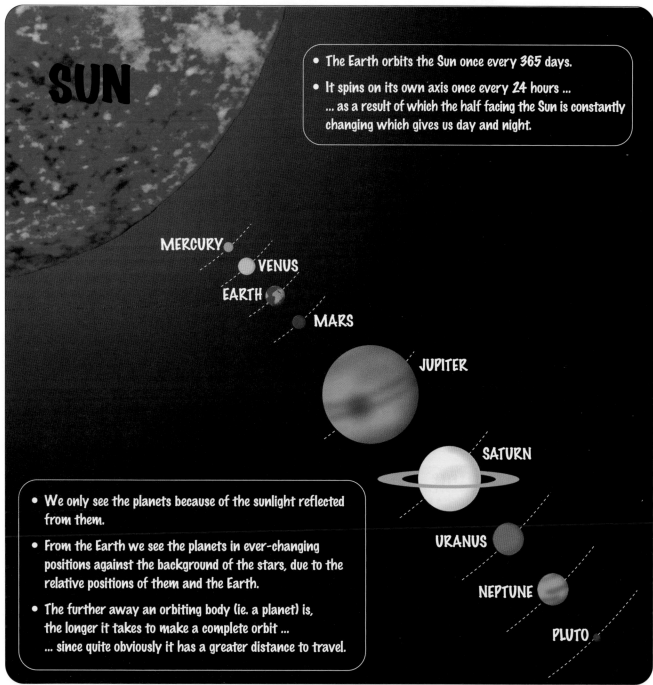

SUN

- The Earth orbits the Sun once every 365 days.
- It spins on its own axis once every 24 hours ...
  ... as a result of which the half facing the Sun is constantly changing which gives us day and night.

MERCURY

VENUS

EARTH

MARS

JUPITER

SATURN

- We only see the planets because of the sunlight reflected from them.
- From the Earth we see the planets in ever-changing positions against the background of the stars, due to the relative positions of them and the Earth.
- The further away an orbiting body (ie. a planet) is, the longer it takes to make a complete orbit ...
  ... since quite obviously it has a greater distance to travel.

URANUS

NEPTUNE

PLUTO

Comets

- They have a CORE of FROZEN GAS and DUST ...
- ... and an ELLIPTICAL ORBIT around the Sun.
- As they approach the Sun ...
- GASES EVAPORATE to form the TAIL ...
- ... making the comet easy to see.

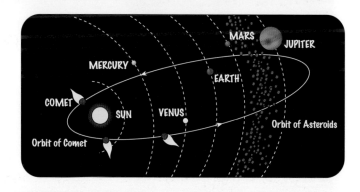

MARS

JUPITER

MERCURY

EARTH

COMET

SUN

VENUS

Orbit of Asteroids

Orbit of Comet

SATELLITES

- A satellite is a smaller object which is in orbit around a much larger object.
- It is kept in this orbit by a combination of ...
  - ... ITS HIGH ORBITING SPEED and ...
  - ... THE FORCE OF GRAVITY BETWEEN THE BODIES.

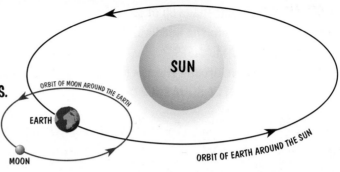

Gravity And Orbiting Speed

As the distance between two bodies <u>increases</u>, there is a proportionally greater <u>decrease</u> in the force of gravity between them ...

If the distance between two objects is doubled the force between them becomes $\frac{1}{4}$ of the original force. Trebling the distance results in $\frac{1}{9}$ th of the force!

This means that to stay in orbit at a particular distance, smaller bodies must orbit at a particular speed, to balance the gravitational force. For satellites at large distances this means orbiting slowly and therefore taking a much longer time to complete an orbit (due to slow speed and huge circumference of orbit!)

Artificial Satellites

These are placed in orbit by scientists to do a particular job ...

❶ OBSERVATION SATELLITES
- These are in orbit ABOVE THE EARTH'S ATMOSPHERE.
- These have TELESCOPES and the SOLAR SYSTEM and beyond can be OBSERVED without ...
- ... any INTERFERENCE from the ATMOSPHERE, CLOUDS and WEATHER STORMS.

❷ COMMUNICATION SATELLITES
- These LINK UP different countries so that ...
- ... RADIO, TV broadcasts and TELEPHONE CALLS ...
- ... can be SENT from ONE COUNTRY TO ANOTHER

❸ MONITORING SATELLITES
- These collect INFORMATION about the ATMOSPHERE ...
- ... including MOVEMENT OF CLOUDS ...
- ... so that WEATHER FORECASTS can be made.

GEOSTATIONARY COMMUNICATION SATELLITES

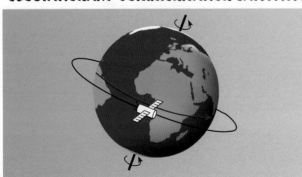

The satellite has an orbit passing high above the equator moving around the Earth at exactly the same rate as the Earth spins ie. it takes 24 hours to complete its orbit. This means that it always stays at the same point above the equator ie. a geostationary orbit. Potential interference with each other's signals means that there is only room for about 400 of these satellites.

POLAR MONITORING SATELLITES

The satellite has a low polar orbit ie. it passes continuously over the North and South poles, so that the Earth spins beneath it. These satellites orbit and scan the Earth several times every day, from a much closer range than a geostationary satellite.

Stars, Galaxies And The Universe

- Our SUN is ONE STAR out of the many millions of stars in OUR GALAXY, THE MILKY WAY.
- The Milky Way is ONE GALAXY out of at least a billion galaxies in the UNIVERSE.

The stars in the night sky stay in fixed patterns (called constellations). Those planets, which are visible to the naked eye, look very much like stars because of the light they reflect. The planets, however, unlike stars, move very slowly across the night sky and therefore change their positions relative to the constellations. Many of these constellations have famous names eg. the plough, because of their shapes.

Formation Of Stars

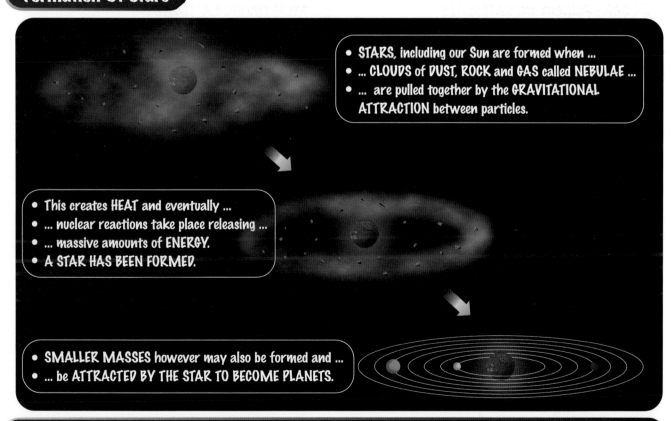

How To Detect Life On Other Planets

Amongst the prime contenders for life in our solar system are MARS and EUROPA (one of Jupiter's satellites). However this life may be fairly basic, such as microbes etc. or their fossilised remains.

OBTAINING EVIDENCE

Actually travel to Mars or Europa and look for signs of life!

Could take 18 months to get to Mars though!

Use robots to travel to Mars or Europa and bring back samples.

Not as reliable as humans!

Use robots to travel to Mars or Europa and take pictures!

Pictures might not come out!

ANALYSING EVIDENCE

Looking for fossilised remains ...
The samples you manage to obtain should be sliced carefully using special equipment. The thin slices can then be analysed using an electron microscope.

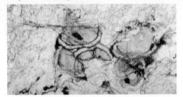

This principle was applied to a meteorite from Mars which was found in the Antarctic. It revealed some bacteria-like structures!!!

Detecting changes produced by living things ...
The samples of rock or dust can be placed inside a sealed container whose atmosphere has been accurately analysed. Over a period of time the atmosphere is checked to see if there are changes which have occurred

which cannot be attributed to chemical or geological processes eg. oxygen could have been used up or produced by living things in the sample.

SETI

Of course it's possible that there may be highly advanced forms of life elsewhere in the universe and these may be detected using radio telescopes to try to find meaningful signals in a narrow waveband against the background 'noise' of the universe. The SEARCH FOR EXTRA-TERRESTRIAL INTELLIGENCE (SETI) has now gone on for more than 40 years without success; but remember the universe is vast and any day now ...

Red-shift

If a SOURCE OF LIGHT (same effect occurs with sound) moves away from us the wavelengths of the light in its spectrum are LONGER than if the source was not moving!!! For light this is known as 'RED-SHIFT' as the wavelengths are 'shifted' TOWARDS THE RED END OF THE SPECTRUM.

The wavelengths of light from other galaxies are longer than expected, which means that ...

... the GALAXY IS MOVING AWAY FROM US VERY QUICKLY ...

... this effect is exaggerated in galaxies which are further away, which means that ...

... the FURTHER AWAY A GALAXY IS, THE FASTER IT IS MOVING AWAY FROM US.

This evidence suggests that the whole universe is expanding and that it might have started billions of years ago, from one place with a 'Big Bang' (a huge explosion!)

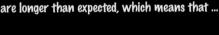

BANG!!

- During the main stable life period of a star the MASSIVE FORCES of ATTRACTION pulling INWARDS ...
  ... are BALANCED by FORCES ACTING OUTWARDS created by the HUGE TEMPERATURES within the star.

Towards the end of the star's life, two different processes may occur ...

STAR

... stars at least 4x bigger than our sun can expand enormously to become RED SUPERGIANTS.

... stars the size of our sun will eventually expand to become a RED GIANT.

RED SUPERGIANT

RED GIANT

SUPERNOVA

The RED SUPERGIANT rapidly ...
... SHRINKS and EXPLODES releasing ...
... MASSIVE AMOUNTS OF ENERGY ...
... and DUST and GAS into space.
This is a SUPERNOVA.

WHITE DWARF

The RED GIANT continues to COOL DOWN ...
... and will eventually COLLAPSE under ...
... its own GRAVITY to become a WHITE DWARF ...
... with a density millions of times greater than any matter on Earth.

NEUTRON STAR

For medium-sized stars, (10x bigger than our sun) the remnants of the supernova form a NEUTRON STAR, formed only of neutrons. A cupful of this matter could have a mass greater than 15,000 million tonnes!!

HIGHER

BLACK HOLE

Those stars greater than 10x the size of our sun are massive enough to leave behind black holes, where the matter is so dense and the gravitational field so strong that nothing can escape from it - not even light or other forms of electromagnetic radiation. Black holes can only be observed indirectly through their effects on their surroundings eg. the X-rays emitted when gases from a nearby star spiral into a black hole.

Recycling Stellar Material

We now know that lighter elements such as hydrogen and helium fuse together to produce NUCLEI of heavier elements during the nuclear fusion reactions which release energy in stars.
But atoms of these heavier elements are also present in the inner planets of the solar system, leading us to believe that the solar system was formed from the material produced when earlier stars exploded.

Waves are a REGULAR PATTERN OF DISTURBANCE
They can be produced in ROPES, SPRINGS and on the SURFACE OF WATER.

Features Of Waves

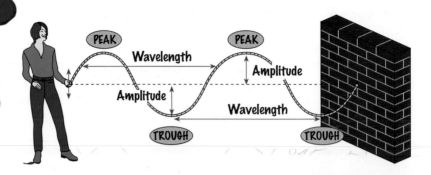

A simple wave can be generated by simply tying one end of a rope to a wall.

PEAK   PEAK
Wavelength
Amplitude
Amplitude
Wavelength
TROUGH   TROUGH

AMPLITUDE is ...	WAVELENGTH is ...	FREQUENCY is ...
... the MAXIMUM DISTURBANCE caused by a wave.	... the DISTANCE BETWEEN CORRESPONDING POINTS ON TWO SUCCESSIVE DISTURBANCES.	... the NUMBER of WAVES PRODUCED, (or passing a particular point) IN ONE SECOND.

Types Of Wave

There are TWO types of wave, both of which can be shown using a SLINKY SPRING.

1. TRANSVERSE WAVES

- The PATTERN OF DISTURBANCE ...
  ... is at RIGHT ANGLES (90°) to ...
  ... the DIRECTION OF WAVE MOVEMENT.

DIRECTION OF WAVE MOVEMENT

HAND MOVES UP AND DOWN

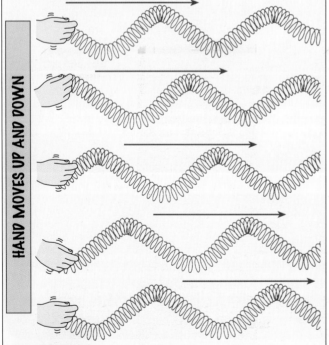

EXAMPLES

- LIGHT which can travel through a vacuum ie. it does not need a medium.
- WATERWAVES
- WAVES IN ROPES

2. LONGITUDINAL WAVES

- The PATTERN OF DISTURBANCE ...
  ... is in the SAME DIRECTION as ...
  ... the DIRECTION OF WAVE MOVEMENT.

DIRECTION OF WAVE MOVEMENT

HAND MOVES BACKWARDS AND FORWARDS

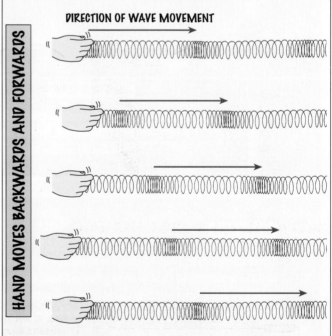

EXAMPLES

- ALL SOUND which can travel through solids, liquids and gases.

Reflection Of Waves

- Waves are REFLECTED when a BARRIER is placed in their path.
- The effect can be seen with waves generated in a ROPE or SPRING ...
- ... and with WATERWAVES.

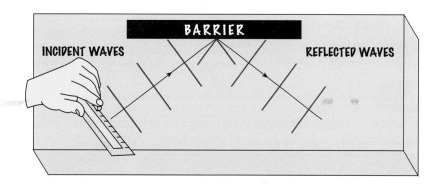

Refraction Of Waves

- When WAVES CROSS A BOUNDARY ...
- ... between ONE MEDIUM AND ANOTHER (OF DIFFERENT DENSITY) ...
- ... there is a CHANGE OF SPEED of the waves ...
- ... which causes the waves to CHANGE DIRECTION ...
- ... unless the waves meet the boundary along a NORMAL (AT 90°).
- With WATERWAVES refraction occurs when the waves pass into DEEPER or SHALLOWER WATER.

WATERWAVES PASSING INTO SHALLOWER WATER

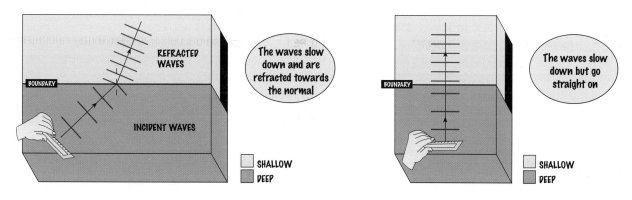

WATERWAVES PASSING INTO DEEPER WATER

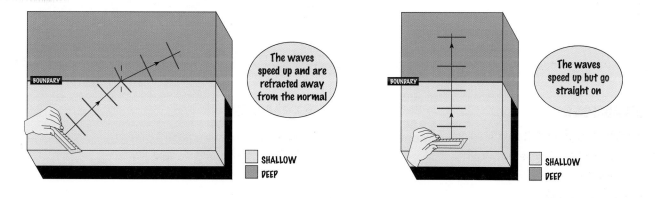

The behaviour of waves shown on the previous page suggests that light and sound (See P.88) also travel as waves and are refracted because they travel at different speeds in different materials (media).

Reflection Of Light

This occurs when light strikes a SURFACE resulting in it CHANGING ITS DIRECTION.
If the surface is perfectly smooth and shiny (eg. a mirror) then the following law of reflection applies ...

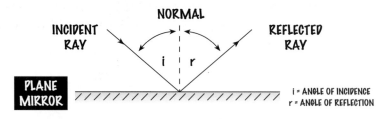

i = ANGLE OF INCIDENCE
r = ANGLE OF REFLECTION

ANGLE OF INCIDENCE   =   ANGLE OF REFLECTION

Refraction Of Light

Light changes direction when it crosses a boundary between two transparent materials (media) of different densities - UNLESS it meets the boundary at an angle of 90° (along a NORMAL).

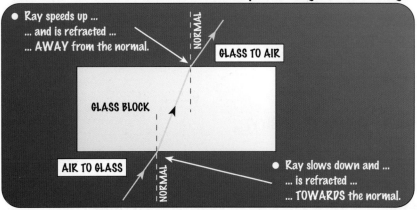

- Ray speeds up ...
  ... and is refracted ...
  ... AWAY from the normal.

GLASS TO AIR

GLASS BLOCK

AIR TO GLASS

- Ray slows down and ...
  ... is refracted ...
  ... TOWARDS the normal.

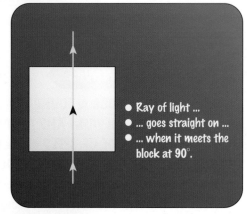

- Ray of light ...
- ... goes straight on ...
- ... when it meets the block at 90°.

Total Internal Reflection – When Refraction Becomes Reflection

When a ray of light travels from glass, 'perspex' or water into air, some light is also reflected from the boundary. This can be best summarised in THREE stages. If the ANGLE OF INCIDENCE is ...

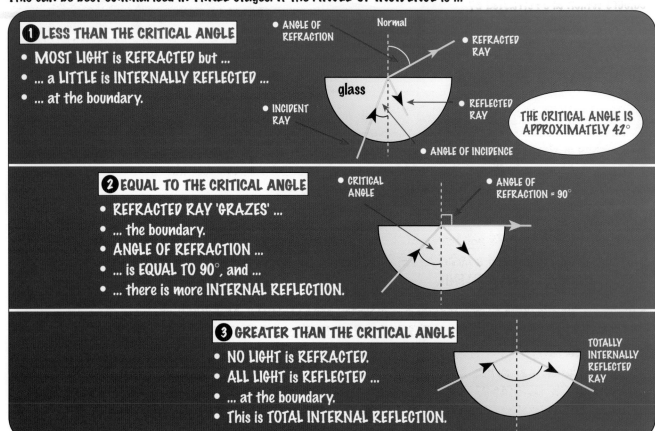

❶ LESS THAN THE CRITICAL ANGLE
- MOST LIGHT is REFRACTED but ...
- ... a LITTLE is INTERNALLY REFLECTED ...
- ... at the boundary.

- ANGLE OF REFRACTION
- Normal
- REFRACTED RAY
- glass
- REFLECTED RAY
- INCIDENT RAY
- ANGLE OF INCIDENCE

THE CRITICAL ANGLE IS APPROXIMATELY 42°

❷ EQUAL TO THE CRITICAL ANGLE
- REFRACTED RAY 'GRAZES' ...
- ... the boundary.
- ANGLE OF REFRACTION ...
- ... is EQUAL TO 90°, and ...
- ... there is more INTERNAL REFLECTION.

- CRITICAL ANGLE
- ANGLE OF REFRACTION = 90°

❸ GREATER THAN THE CRITICAL ANGLE
- NO LIGHT is REFRACTED.
- ALL LIGHT is REFLECTED ...
- ... at the boundary.
- This is TOTAL INTERNAL REFLECTION.

TOTALLY INTERNALLY REFLECTED RAY

Light is one type of ELECTROMAGNETIC RADIATION, which together with the other various types form a continuous range called the ELECTROMAGNETIC SPECTRUM. The seven 'colours of the rainbow' form the visible spectrum, which as the name suggests is the only part of the electromagnetic spectrum that we can see. Electromagnetic radiation can be REFLECTED and REFRACTED which supports the idea that they travel as WAVES.

Types Of Electromagnetic Radiation In The Electromagnetic Spectrum

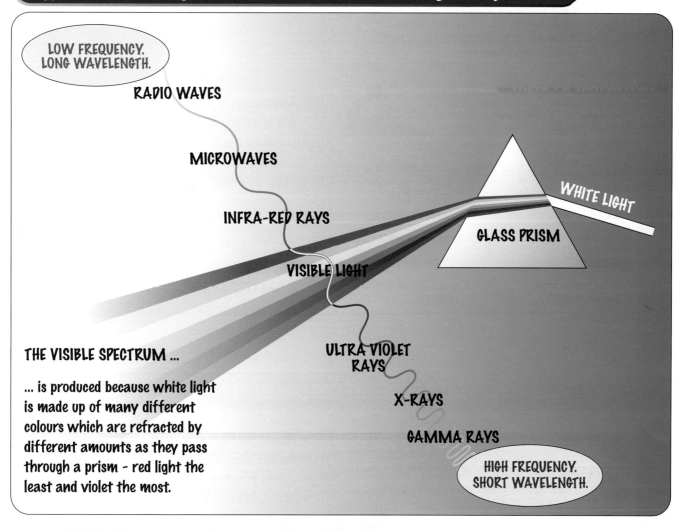

LOW FREQUENCY. LONG WAVELENGTH.

RADIO WAVES

MICROWAVES

INFRA-RED RAYS

VISIBLE LIGHT

WHITE LIGHT

GLASS PRISM

ULTRA VIOLET RAYS

X-RAYS

GAMMA RAYS

HIGH FREQUENCY. SHORT WAVELENGTH.

THE VISIBLE SPECTRUM ...

... is produced because white light is made up of many different colours which are refracted by different amounts as they pass through a prism - red light the least and violet the most.

Characteristics Of Electromagnetic Radiation

• Each type of electromagnetic radiation ...
1. TRAVELS AT THE SAME SPEED (300,000,000m/s) THROUGH SPACE (a vacuum).
2. Has a DIFFERENT WAVELENGTH and a DIFFERENT FREQUENCY.

> RADIO WAVES, MICROWAVES and INFRA-RED RAYS <u>ALL</u> have a LONGER WAVELENGTH and a LOWER FREQUENCY compared to VISIBLE LIGHT.

> ULTRA VIOLET RAYS, X-RAYS and GAMMA RAYS <u>ALL</u> have a SHORTER WAVELENGTH and a HIGHER FREQUENCY compared to VISIBLE LIGHT.

• Different wavelengths of electromagnetic radiation are REFLECTED, ABSORBED, or TRANSMITTED DIFFERENTLY by DIFFERENT SUBSTANCES and TYPE OF SURFACE eg. Black surfaces are particularly good absorbers of infra-red radiation.
• When radiation is absorbed, the energy it carries ...
   ... MAKES THE SUBSTANCE WHICH ABSORBS IT HOTTER, ...
   ... MAY CREATE AN ALTERNATING CURRENT WITH THE SAME FREQUENCY AS THE RADIATION.
This principle is used in TV and radio aerials to receive information via radio waves.

Uses Of Electromagnetic Waves

Effects Of Electromagnetic Waves

RADIO WAVES

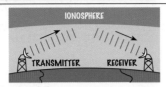

IONOSPHERE
TRANSMITTER   RECEIVER

- Transmit Radio and TV programmes between different places. The longer wavelength radio waves are reflected ...
  ... from the ionosphere, an electrically charged layer ...
  ... in the Earth's upper atmosphere.

- This means that long wave radio waves can be sent between different points despite the fact that the Earth's surface curves.

MICROWAVES

- Satellite communication and mobile phone networks since they can pass easily through the Earth's atmosphere.

- Cooking, because microwaves are ...
- ... absorbed by water molecules ...
- ... causing them to heat up.

- Microwaves are dangerous because they are absorbed by water in cells ...
  ... where the heat released ...
  ... may DAMAGE or KILL CELLS.
  Correct care must be taken in the use of microwaves.

INFRA-RED RAYS

- Grills, toasters and radiant heaters.
- Optical Fibre communication.

- Remote control for TV ...
  ... and VCR's.

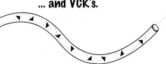

- Absorbed by skin ...
  ... and FELT as HEAT.
  Excessive amount can cause BURNS.

VISIBLE SPECTRUM (See P.85)

ULTRA VIOLET RAYS

- For suntanning and sunbeds.

- Fluorescent lamp & security coding ...
  ... where surface coated with special paint ...
  ... absorbs U-V and emits visible LIGHT.

- Passes through skin to the TISSUES below. Darker skin allows less penetration ...
  ... and provides more protection.
- HIGH DOSES of this ionising radiation can KILL NORMAL CELLS ...
  ... and a LOW DOSE can cause CANCER.

X-RAYS

- Produce shadow pictures of ...
  ... BONES and METALS, ...
  ... materials X-rays do not easily pass through.

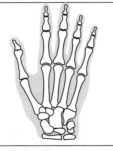

- Pass through SOFT TISSUES ...
  ... although SOME is ABSORBED.
- As for U-V ...
  ... HIGH DOSES of this ionising radiation can KILL NORMAL CELLS ...
  ... and LOW DOSES can cause CANCER.

GAMMA RAYS

- Killing cancer cells.

- Killing bacteria on food ...
  ... and surgical instruments.

- Pass through SOFT TISSUES ...
  ... although SOME is ABSORBED.
- As for U-V and X-Rays ...
  ... HIGH DOSES of this ionising radiation can KILL NORMAL CELLS ...
  ... and LOW DOSES can cause CANCER.

Sound eg. speech or music can be sent long distances if it is converted into electrical signals ...

 A microphone in the mouthpiece converts sound into electrical signals which pass down the wire. These electrical signals match the frequency and amplitude of the sound waves.

These electrical signals can then be sent using ...

... CABLES.
Copper cables suffer from weakening of the signal during transmission.
To boost the signal regular amplification of the signal is required.

... ELECTROMAGNETIC WAVES.
Here a radio wave is used to 'carry' the electrical signal from a transmitter ...

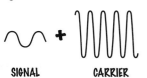
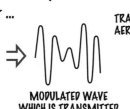

SIGNAL CARRIER MODULATED WAVE WHICH IS TRANSMITTED

TRANSMITTER AERIAL

RECEIVING AERIAL

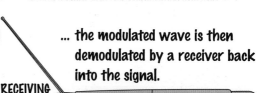

... the modulated wave is then demodulated by a receiver back into the signal.

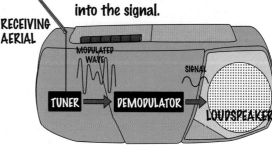

MODULATED WAVE SIGNAL

TUNER → DEMODULATOR → LOUDSPEAKER

Optical Fibres

Information can also be transmitted using OPTICAL FIBRES where the electrical signal is converted into light or infra red pulses.

More information can be sent this way than by sending electrical signals through cables of the same diameter, with less weakening of signal strength along the way.

Analogue And Digital Signals

- Analogue signals vary continually in amplitude and/or frequency. They are very similar to the sound waves of speech or music.

- Digital signals on the other hand do not vary and they have only two states, ON (I) or OFF (O). There are no inbetween states. The information is a series of pulses.

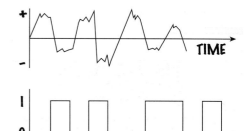

+
-
TIME

I
0
TIME

An advantage of using a digital signal instead of an analogue signal is better quality, with no change in the signal information during transmission.

Why Digital Is Better Than Analogue

Transmitted signals become weaker. They may also pick up additional signals or noise. At selective intervals the transmitted signals have to be amplified.

- Different frequencies within analogue signals weaken by different amounts. When amplified these differences and any noise which has been picked up results in the signal becoming less and less like the original signal ie. there is a deterioration in quality.

- Digital signals also weaken during transmission. However, the pulses are still recognisable as 'ON' or 'OFF'. Noise doesn't affect digital signals since it usually has a low amplitude which is recognised as an 'OFF' state. When amplified the quality of the digital signal is retained.

 ⇒  ⇒

TRANSMITTED SIGNAL DETERIORATED SIGNAL AMPLIFIED SIGNAL

SOUND ...
- ... is produced when something VIBRATES backwards and forwards.
- It is REFLECTED from HARD SURFACES, these reflections are called ECHOES and ...
- ... is REFRACTED when it passes into a DIFFERENT MEDIUM or SUBSTANCE.

Since sound can be reflected and refracted this provides evidence that SOUND TRAVELS AS WAVES.

Representing Sound On An Oscilloscope Trace

It is possible for us to 'see' a representation of a sound wave if we connect a signal generator to an oscilloscope

A SIGNAL GENERATOR can generate sound waves whose PITCH and LOUDNESS can be changed.

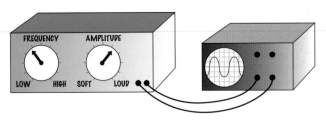

The OSCILLOSCOPE displays a representation of the sound wave on its screen, as a trace.

Frequency And Pitch

The FREQUENCY is the NUMBER OF VIBRATIONS PRODUCED in ONE SECOND. It is measured in HERTZ, Hz. The HIGHER the FREQUENCY of the sound waves, the HIGHER the PITCH of the sound. A change in frequency can be represented on the oscilloscope screen, if the frequency dial of the signal generator is turned.

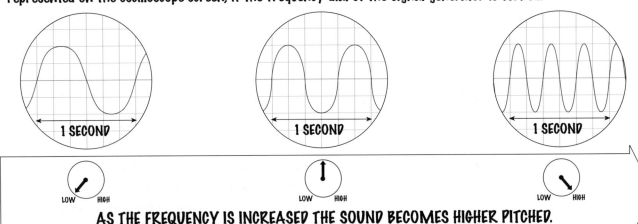

AS THE FREQUENCY IS INCREASED THE SOUND BECOMES HIGHER PITCHED.

Amplitude And Loudness

AMPLITUDE is the BIGGEST MOVEMENT OF THE VIBRATING OBJECT FROM ITS REST POSITION.
The GREATER the AMPLITUDE of the sound waves the GREATER the LOUDNESS of the sound. A change in amplitude can be represented on the oscilloscope screen if the amplitude dial on the signal generator is turned.

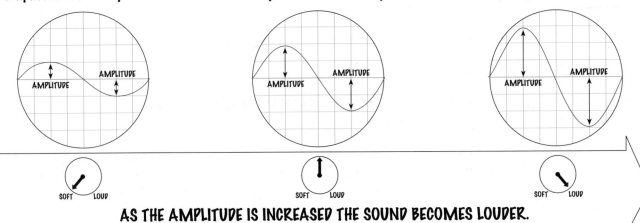

AS THE AMPLITUDE IS INCREASED THE SOUND BECOMES LOUDER.

These are SOUND WAVES of FREQUENCIES GREATER than 20,000 Hz ie. above the UPPER LIMIT of the HEARING RANGE for HUMANS. They are made by ELECTRONIC SYSTEMS which produce ELECTRICAL OSCILLATIONS which are used to generate the ULTRASONIC WAVES.

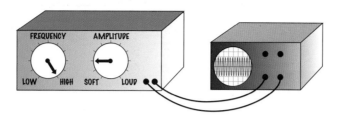

They have many uses ...

1. Pre-natal Scanning

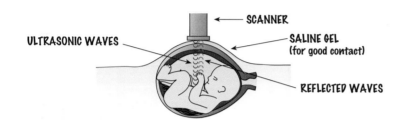

THIS METHOD IS SAFE WITH NO RISK TO PATIENT OR BABY.

2. Detecting Flaws And Cracks

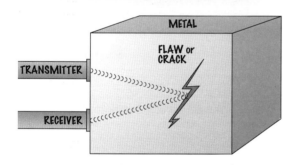

• Some of the ultrasound waves are reflected back by the flaw or crack within the structure.

3. Cleaning Delicate Objects

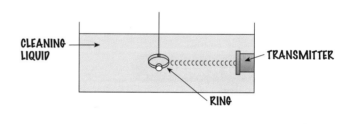

• The vibrations caused by the ultrasound waves dislodge dirt particles from the surface of the object.

HOW THEY WORK

• Ultrasonic waves are PARTLY REFLECTED ...
• ... at the BOUNDARY as they pass from ...
• ... ONE MEDIUM or SUBSTANCE into another one.
• The TIME TAKEN for these REFLECTIONS is a ...
• ... measure of the DEPTH of the REFLECTING SURFACE and ...
• ... the reflected waves are usually PROCESSED ...
• ... to produce a VISUAL IMAGE on a SCREEN.

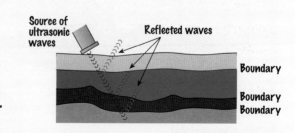

• Ultrasonic waves can also be used within a LIQUID to CLEAN DELICATE OBJECTS where ...
• ... the VIBRATIONS DISLODGE DIRT PARTICLES ...
• ... from the SURFACE of the object.
• Using this method means there is ...
• ... NO DANGER OF BREAKAGE or ...
• ... need to DISASSEMBLE the object.

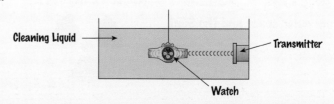

Some substances give out radiation all the time, regardless of what is done to them. These substances are said to be RADIOACTIVE.

This process involves a change in the structure of the radioactive atom and the release of one of the three types of radiation.

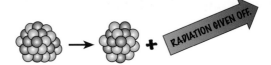

RADIATION GIVEN OFF.

The Three Types Of Radiation

A radioactive substance is capable of emitting one of the following types of radiation, ALPHA, BETA or GAMMA. A simple way to distinguish between them is by their ability to be absorbed by different types of material.

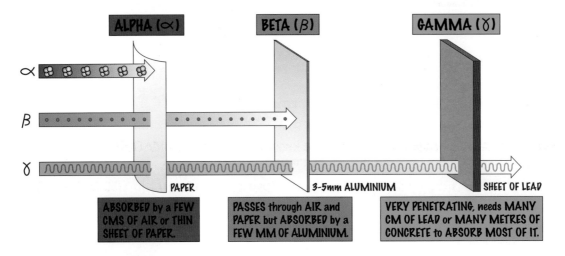

ALPHA (∝)   BETA (β)   GAMMA (γ)

∝

β

γ

PAPER   3-5mm ALUMINIUM   SHEET OF LEAD

ABSORBED by a FEW CMS OF AIR or THIN SHEET OF PAPER.

PASSES through AIR and PAPER but ABSORBED by a FEW MM OF ALUMINIUM.

VERY PENETRATING, needs MANY CM OF LEAD or MANY METRES OF CONCRETE to ABSORB MOST OF IT.

Background Radiation

This is RADIATION THAT OCCURS NATURALLY ALL AROUND US. It only provides a very small dose ALTOGETHER so there's no danger to our health.

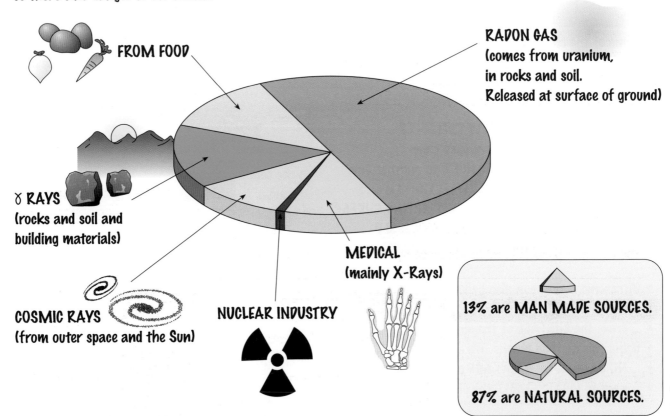

FROM FOOD

RADON GAS
(comes from uranium, in rocks and soil. Released at surface of ground)

γ RAYS
(rocks and soil and building materials)

MEDICAL
(mainly X-Rays)

COSMIC RAYS
(from outer space and the Sun)

NUCLEAR INDUSTRY

13% are MAN MADE SOURCES.

87% are NATURAL SOURCES.

As we said on the previous page, we are all exposed to some degree of radiation. This is BACKGROUND RADIATION and because the dosage is small there's very little, if any, danger to health. However, prolonged exposure to some types of radiation can result in health risks, and steps must be taken to limit the exposure of people in high risk jobs within the nuclear industry.

Ionisation

- When RADIATION COLLIDES with NEUTRAL ATOMS or MOLECULES ...
  ... they may become CHARGED due to electrons being 'knocked out' of their structure
  This alters their structure leaving them as IONS or CHARGED PARTICLES.

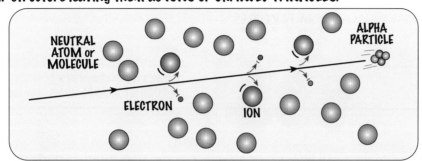

- ALPHA, BETA and GAMMA radiation are therefore known as IONISING RADIATION ...
  ... and can damage 'healthy' MOLECULES in LIVING CELLS resulting in death of the cell.
- One beneficial effect of ionising radiation is that higher doses of it can be used to KILL CANCER CELLS and HARMFUL MICROORGANISMS.

Acute Dangers

Damage to cells in organs can cause CANCER.
The larger the dose of radiation the greater the risk of cancer. However, the damaging effect depends on whether the radiation source is INSIDE or OUTSIDE the body.

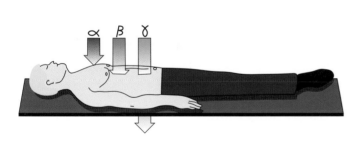

If the source is OUTSIDE ...
- ∝ CANNOT PENETRATE THE BODY and is stopped by the skin.
- β and δ CAN PENETRATE THE BODY to reach the CELLS of ORGANS and be absorbed by them.

If the source is INSIDE ...
- ∝ causes MOST DAMAGE as it is STRONGLY ABSORBED BY CELLS causing the MOST IONISATION.
- β and δ cause LESS DAMAGE as they are less likely to be absorbed by cells.

Detecting Radiation Before The Damage Is Done

Workers who work in the nuclear industry and are regularly exposed to radiation often wear a badge to monitor their degree of exposure. The badge contains photographic film, which after developing, becomes darker the more radiation it has been exposed to.

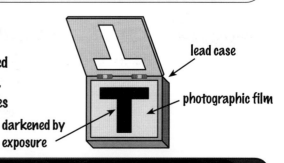

lead case

photographic film

darkened by exposure

Rutherford And Marsden

A LONG TIME AGO ...

- ... it was thought that the ATOM was a SPHERE of POSITIVE CHARGE ...
- ... with NEGATIVELY CHARGED ELECTRONS spread through it like a 'PLUM PUDDING'!!

AT THE BEGINNING OF THIS CENTURY ...

- ... Rutherford and Marsden performed the SCATTERING EXPERIMENT where VERY THIN GOLD FOIL (a few atoms thick) ...
- ... was BOMBARDED by ALPHA ($\propto$) PARTICLES which were known to have a POSITIVE CHARGE.

ALPHA PARTICLES

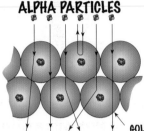

- Most $\propto$ particles PASSED STRAIGHT THROUGH or were DEFLECTED BY A SMALL AMOUNT. However ...

... some $\propto$ particles were ...
... DEFLECTED BACK TOWARDS THE SOURCE ...
... proving the existence of a CONCENTRATED REGION ...
... of POSITIVE CHARGE which they called the NUCLEUS.

GOLD ATOM

These results led us to the modern day view of the structure of the atom which is that ...
... the ATOM consists of a small CENTRAL NUCLEUS made up of PROTONS and NEUTRONS (one exception!) ...
... surrounded by ELECTRONS arranged in SHELLS.

A Simple Example – Helium

PROTON
- Positively charged.
- An atom has the same number of protons as electrons ...
  ... so the atom as a whole has no electrical charge.
- Same mass as a neutron.

NEUTRON
- Neutral - no charge.
- Same mass as a proton.

ELECTRON
- Negatively charged.
- Same number of electrons as protons.
- Mass negligible ie. nearly nothing!

ATOMIC PARTICLE	RELATIVE MASS	RELATIVE CHARGE
PROTON	1	+1
NEUTRON	1	0
ELECTRON	0 (nearly!)	-1

Mass Number And Proton Number

Atoms of an element can be described very conveniently; take the Helium atom above ...

MASS NUMBER (Nucleon Number) ⟶ 4
NUMBER OF PROTONS AND NEUTRONS.

ELEMENT SYMBOL
IN THIS CASE, THE ELEMENT HELIUM.

He

PROTON NUMBER ⟶ 2
NUMBER OF PROTONS. This is unique to each individual element.

Here are some more elements in the periodic table.

HYDROGEN, $^{1}_{1}H$

BORON, $^{11}_{5}B$

SODIUM, $^{23}_{11}Na$

| 1 PROTON |
| 0 NEUTRONS (the exception) |
| 1 ELECTRON |

| 5 PROTONS |
| 6 NEUTRONS |
| 5 ELECTRONS |

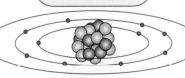

| 11 PROTONS |
| 12 NEUTRONS |
| 11 ELECTRONS |

Isotopes

- ALL ATOMS of a particular ELEMENT have the SAME NUMBER OF PROTONS.
- The NUMBER of PROTONS DEFINES THE ELEMENT.
    - HOWEVER, some atoms of the SAME ELEMENT can have DIFFERENT NUMBERS OF NEUTRONS ...
        - ... these are called ISOTOPES.

EXAMPLE:

Oxygen has 3 isotopes ...

$^{16}_{8}O$ ... has 8 NEUTRONS ... $^{17}_{8}O$ ... has 9 NEUTRONS ... $^{18}_{8}O$ ... has 10 NEUTRONS ...

Radioactive isotopes (RADIOISOTOPES or RADIONUCLIDES) are atoms with unstable nuclei which may disintegrate emitting radiation and causing the formation of a different atom with a different number of protons.
This is RADIOACTIVE DECAY and the amount of radiation emitted by a particular radioactive material depends on its AGE. The OLDER IT IS THE LESS RADIATION IT EMITS.

1. Alpha (α) Emission

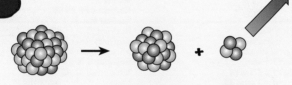

UNSTABLE NUCLEUS   NEW NUCLEUS   ALPHA α PARTICLE

- The original atom decays by ejecting an ALPHA (α) PARTICLE from the NUCLEUS.
- This particle is a HELIUM NUCLEUS, a particle made up of TWO PROTONS and TWO NEUTRONS.
- A NEW ATOM IS FORMED with α decay.

2. Beta (β) Emission

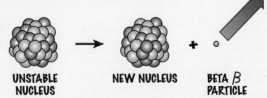

UNSTABLE NUCLEUS   NEW NUCLEUS   BETA β PARTICLE

- The original atom decays by changing a NEUTRON into a PROTON and an ELECTRON!
- This HIGH ENERGY ELECTRON which is now EJECTED from the nucleus ...
- ... is a BETA (β) PARTICLE.
- A NEW ATOM IS FORMED with β decay.

3. Gamma (γ) Emission

ALPHA α PARTICLE

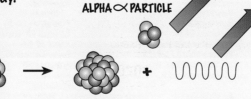

UNSTABLE NUCLEUS   STABLE NUCLEUS   GAMMA γ RADIATION

- After α or β DECAY a nucleus sometimes contains SURPLUS ENERGY.
- It emits this as GAMMA (γ) RADIATION which is ...
- ... VERY HIGH FREQUENCY ELECTROMAGNETIC RADIATION.
- Unlike α or β decay this in itself has NO EFFECT ON THE STRUCTURE OF THE NUCLEUS.

Hazard Symbols

Hazard	Symbol	Examples	Dealing with Spillage
Oxidising substances provide oxygen which allows other materials to burn more fiercely		Potassium Chlorate	Wear eye protection. Scoop the solid into a dry bucket. Rinse the area with water.
Highly Flammable substances easily catch fire.		Ethanol	Shut off all possible sources of heat or ignition. Open all windows to ventilate the area. Soak up the ethanol and dilute with water.
Toxic substances can cause death. They may have their effects when swallowed or breathed in or absorbed through the skin.		Chlorine	Evacuate the laboratory! Open a few outside windows to ventilate the room. Keep all internal doors closed.
Harmful substances are similar to toxic substances but less dangerous.		Iodine	Wear eye protection and gloves. Clear the iodine into a fume cupboard and add to sodium thiosulphate solution.
Corrosive substances attack and destroy living tissues, including eyes and skin.		1. Hydrochloric Acid 2. Sodium Hydroxide	1. Wear eye protection. Neutralise with sodium carbonate. Rinse area. 2. Wear eye protection. Neutralise with citric acid. Rinse area.
Irritants are not corrosive but can cause reddening or blistering of the skin.		Calcium Chloride	Wear eye protection. Scoop up solid and dissolve in water.

* Please note some spillages will be dealt with by laboratory technicians or teachers.

The Periodic Table

Key

Mass number → 1

H hydrogen

Atomic number (Proton number) → 1

8 or 0

1	2											3	4	5	6	7	4 He helium 2
7 Li lithium 3	9 Be beryllium 4											11 B boron 5	12 C carbon 6	14 N nitrogen 7	16 O oxygen 8	19 F fluorine 9	20 Ne neon 10
23 Na sodium 11	24 Mg magnesium 12											27 Al aluminium 13	28 Si silicon 14	31 P phosphorus 15	32 S sulphur 16	35 Cl chlorine 17	40 Ar argon 18
39 K potassium 19	40 Ca calcium 20	45 Sc scandium 21	48 Ti titanium 22	51 V vanadium 23	52 Cr chromium 24	55 Mn manganese 25	56 Fe iron 26	59 Co cobalt 27	59 Ni nickel 28	63 Cu copper 29	64 Zn zinc 30	70 Ga gallium 31	73 Ge germanium 32	75 As arsenic 33	79 Se selenium 34	80 Br bromine 35	84 Kr krypton 36
85 Rb rubidium 37	88 Sr strontium 38	89 Y yttrium 39	91 Zr zirconium 40	93 Nb niobium 41	96 Mo molybdenum 42	98 Tc technetium 43	101 Ru ruthenium 44	103 Rh rhodium 45	106 Pd palladium 46	108 Ag silver 47	112 Cd cadmium 48	115 In indium 49	119 Sn tin 50	122 Sb antimony 51	128 Te tellurium 52	127 I iodine 53	131 Xe xenon 54
133 Cs caesium 55	137 Ba barium 56	139 La lanthanum 57	178 Hf hafnium 72	181 Ta tantalum 73	184 W tungsten 74	186 Re rhenium 75	190 Os osmium 76	192 Ir iridium 77	195 Pt platinum 78	197 Au gold 79	201 Hg mercury 80	204 Tl thallium 81	207 Pb lead 82	209 Bi bismuth 83	210 Po polonium 84	210 At astatine 85	222 Rn radon 86
223 Fr francium 87	226 Ra radium 88	227 Ac actinium 89															

140 Ce cerium 58	141 Pr praseodymium 59	144 Nd neodymium 60	147 Pm promethium 61	150 Sm samarium 62	152 Eu europium 63	157 Gd gadolinium 64	159 Tb terbium 65	162 Dy dysprosium 66	165 Ho holmium 67	167 Er erbium 68	169 Tm thulium 69	173 Yb ytterbium 70	175 Lu lutetium 71
232 Th thorium 90	231 Pa protactinium 91	238 U uranium 92	237 Np neptunium 93	242 Pu plutonium 94	243 Am americium 95	247 Cm curium 96	247 Bk berkelium 97	251 Cf californium 98	254 Es einsteinium 99	253 Fm fermium 100	256 Md mendelevium 101	254 No nobelium 102	257 Lw lawrencium 103

→ The lines of elements going across are called **periods**.

↓ The columns of elements going down are called **groups**.

All you need for **AQA** <u>**Coordinated**</u> **Science Specifications.**

The **Revision Guides ...**
... for **Double Award** and **Separate Sciences**

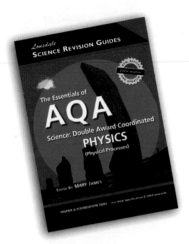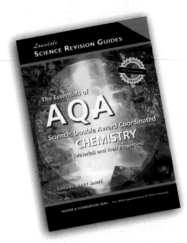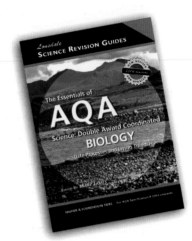

HIGHER AND FOUNDATION TIERS COMBINED

The **Student Worksheets ...**
... for **Double Award** and **Separate Sciences**

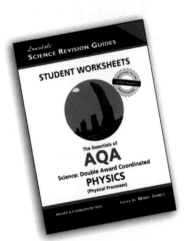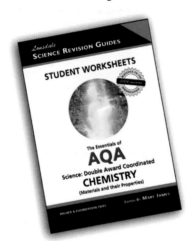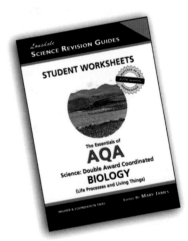

MATCHED PAGE FOR PAGE TO THE REVISION GUIDE

The **Additional Material ...**
... for **Separate Sciences**

- Although written in a modular form it contains all the material, and nothing more, which is needed by a pupil doing separate sciences using the COORDINATED SPECIFICATION

Word equations for making salts

Name Jason Milburn. **Class** _____

A salt is formed when an acid reacts with an alkali. The first part of the name of the salt comes from the name of the metal in the alkali. The second part of the name comes from the name of the acid.

For example, when potassium sulphate is made:

The <u>potassium</u> comes from the <u>potassium</u> hydroxide; the *sulphate* comes from the *sulph*uric acid.

The word equation for this reaction is

potassium hydroxide + sulphuric acid → potassium sulphate + water

Different acids form different salts.

chlorides	are made from	hydrochloric acid
sulphates	are made from	sulphuric acid
nitrates	are made from	nitric acid

? Use the table to help you write word equations like the one above for the following reactions:

1 Potassium hydroxide reacting with sulphuric acid.

potassium hydroxid + sulp. acid → potassium Sulphate + water

2 Potassium hydroxide reacting with nitric acid.

p   hy + n   a → Potassium nitrate + Water.

3 Potassium hydroxide reacting with hydrochloric acid.

_____ _____ + _____ _____ → Potassium chlorids + water.

4 Calcium hydroxide reacting with hydrochloric acid.

Calcium hydroxide + hydrochloric acid → Calcium Chlorids + water.

5 Magnesium oxide reacting with hydrochloric acid.

Magnesium Oxide + hydrochloric acid → Magnesium chlorids + Water.

6 Calcium hydroxide reacting with sulphuric acid.

Calcium hydroxide + Sulphuric acid → Calcium Sulphates + Water.

S knowledge